One-Minute
Mindfulness

How to Live in the Moment

SIMON PARKE

HAY HOUSE

Carlsbad, California • New York City • London • Sydney
Johannesburg • Vancouver • Hong Kong • New Delhi

First published and distributed in the United Kingdom by:
Hay House UK Ltd, Astley House, 33 Notting Hill Gate, London W11 3JQ
Tel: +44 (0)20 3675 2450; Fax: +44 (0)20 3675 2451; www.hayhouse.co.uk

Published and distributed in the United States of America by:
Hay House Inc., PO Box 5100, Carlsbad, CA 92018-5100
Tel: (1) 760 431 7695 or (800) 654 5126
Fax: (1) 760 431 6948 or (800) 650 5115; www.hayhouse.com

Published and distributed in Australia by:
Hay House Australia Ltd, 18/36 Ralph St, Alexandria NSW 2015
Tel: (61) 2 9669 4299; Fax: (61) 2 9669 4144; www.hayhouse.com.au

Published and distributed in the Republic of South Africa by:
Hay House SA (Pty) Ltd, PO Box 990, Witkoppen 2068
info@hayhouse.co.za; www.hayhouse.co.za

Published and distributed in India by:
Hay House Publishers India, Muskaan Complex, Plot No.3, B-2,
Vasant Kunj, New Delhi 110 070
Tel: (91) 11 4176 1620; Fax: (91) 11 4176 1630; www.hayhouse.co.in

Distributed in Canada by:
Raincoast Books, 2440 Viking Way, Richmond, B.C. V6V 1N2
Tel: (1) 604 448 7100; Fax: (1) 604 270 7161; www.raincoast.com

A catalogue record for this book is available from the British Library.

ISBN: 978-1-78180-496-4

Printed in the United States of America

Contents

Introduction

Everyone is talking about mindfulness these days, in a manner I'd never have predicted when the first edition of this book was published.

I'm now asked to take mindfulness into businesses and schools; there are even big articles about it in *The Financial Times*.

Times have changed.

So maybe it's a good moment to go back to basics and remind ourselves of the essence of this practice, which is a triangle (the strongest structure) of inner states, each supporting the other.

Mindfulness is awareness of your present experience with acceptance.

Here is its heartbeat, and in the pages that follow we'll be looking after this heart.

We'll ponder the three points of the triangle:

1. Awareness of yourself and the world

2. Living in the present and

3. Acceptance of your situation (which strangely is the catalyst for good change.)

In other words, how to live in the moment.

Mindfulness is simple, as easily grasped by children as adults; but simple can be hard for distracted minds. So be kind to yourself along the way.

This is no mindfulness text book; those already exist, and wonderfully.

Instead, I offer mindful stories and thoughts for when you sense the need for psychological or emotional shift in your life. Read them once, and then read again... allow them to soak into your consciousness.

We do not have to be anxious, fearful or depressed; and the start of our healing might be to notice that we are.

So welcome to these pages. The journey home to mindful living – aware and present – starts when you want it to.

1

BECOMING
SIMPLE

*Ways to be simple when our
tendency is to be simplistic.
The two are not the same.*

In Search of the Unborn

Perhaps it is a strange place to start, but let there be something of the unborn in us today; for there, in that fragility, is our essence – eternal and undying.

Trapped momentarily in time, we can lose touch with our essence and become children of multiplicity and distraction. We obsess over scraps of knowledge; we seek mastery of many things and worship broken images of truth.

Unborn, we were not so distracted but simple and without boundaries.

So, today, we take into our born lives something of the unborn. Into our multiplicity, we take simplicity; and into the world of competitive knowledge, we take poverty of knowing.

Today we take the deep
unknowing of the unborn.

Present State

Perhaps the most basic teaching of the wisdom school is that our experience of truth is dependent on our state rather than our studies.

In the dawning of light in our lives, there can be no cheating or short cuts. Eight hours a day spent cramming mindfulness techniques in a library won't advance us an inch, for that is all about impatience and all about rush; and, as Philip Booth reminds us in his poem 'Heading Out', 'How you get there is where you'll arrive.'

If rush and impatience is your manner of spiritual travel, don't expect to arrive anywhere beautiful.

Instead, we are mindful of our state, for this alone determines our capacity to receive. 'As our level of being increases,' wrote Maurice Nicoll, a British psychiatrist and teacher of the Fourth Way, 'receptivity to higher meaning increases. As our being decreases, the old meanings return.'

As you listen to your breathing now, allow your present state to become apparent.

Three to Notice

Buddha saw three attitudes as particularly unhelpful for mindful living.

The first is greed, defined as a grabby reaching out for something or a clinging on to it. It's a craving, an attachment to the desired thing.

And its opposite is generosity or renunciation.

The second is hatred, defined as ill-will, judgmental thoughts or aversion to another. It is a pushing away of something deemed undesirable; or an attack on it.

And the opposite of hatred is human friendliness or the spacious absence of hate.

The third unhelpful attitude is delusion, which is the narrow knowing of ignorance or a puffed-up belief in our own knowledge; a belief that we see the whole picture, when in truth we glimpse only certain aspects of reality.

And the opposite of delusion is wisdom, which knows how little can be known.

We joyfully note these attitudes
as they arise in us today.

The Sensible Dog

I once saw a dog jump off a high cliff; it was running one minute, gone the next and it was very shocking.

It was a greyhound, recently retired, and was being taken for a walk by its new owners. Unfortunately, what was obvious to them was not obvious to their pet. Previously, the dog had known only the safe world of cages and racetracks; consequently, it knew very little about freedom and nothing about cliffs.

Even, presuming the dog understood English, were someone to have said, 'Don't jump off the cliff, you'll fall,' it would have been nonsensical to the dog. Given the dog's previous experience of life, and the understanding created by this experience, the idea of 'falling' would have had no meaning. With this mindset, jumping off the cliff was entirely sensible, even though it wasn't.

Remarkably, this story had a happy ending: the dog survived. But a truth about canine and human judgements still hung in the air...

When a proposition sounds stupid, it may be that we are more stupid than the proposition.

Base Camp for Mindfulness

Just as there are many ways to approach the summit of Mount Everest, there are many ways to approach the truths of mindfulness.

But if we were to make a base camp from which to explore, I would choose this one: 'Mindfulness is awareness of present experience with acceptance and trust.'

Staying true to this simple definition of mindfulness, allows us to explore the vast and wonderful mountain that is our present experience.

For now, we note only that mindfulness is not concerned with stale things, past happenings or old perceptions in which many are trapped.

Rather, it is an invitation to fresh experience and virgin knowing, in which present thoughts and emotions are allowed to speak without judgement or rejection.

This element of acceptance helps our wellbeing. Our psyche longs to be healed; and when it realizes that nothing it reveals will cause distress, it tends to reveal all.

A child has so much truth to tell
when they feel no fear.

What to Do about Architectural Disasters

I've decided to dismantle my house. It hasn't been an easy decision, because I've been here a long time and home is home, but I've become increasingly aware of its shortcomings and when I discovered who built it, everything was explained.

My house was built by a partnership called Desire and Ignorance; they often work together, and always with disastrous consequences. It's surprising they aren't more talked of in the press.

They are great survivors but incompetent builders. Desire is famous only for pursuing pleasure and avoiding pain, while Ignorance casts a veil over all his unexamined assumptions and makes wrong ones every hour. Together, they created the psychological reality where I live. Hardly a surprise, therefore, if it's unfit for purpose!

All is not lost, however, because I'm not compelled to live here. I've been here a long time but I'm not a prisoner. I can remove the various layers of brick, wood and plasterboard and create a new space.

It may be hard work, but worth it. In fact, having told you of my intentions, I feel better already.

Mindfulness sometimes talks
about undoing ourselves.

Is This an Alien?

Opening up the shop in the morning and turning the key, I am aware that I am opening up the shop in the morning and turning the key.

Looking at the clouds in their shifting patterns, I am aware that I am looking at the clouds in their shifting patterns.

Becoming irritated by the traffic jam and approaching the end of my tether, I am aware that I'm becoming irritated by the traffic jam and approaching the end of my tether.

This is mindfulness; and it's not complex or alien to us.

Changing State

Mindful meditation has a distinctive feature: it has little or no interest in our thinking.

So, as we settle with our breathing today, our desire is not to think more but to think less. Indeed, we will watch our thoughts passing through, as we might watch drunks passing in the night.

As you allow yourself to fall in with your breathing, you find yourself, perhaps, thinking critically about a colleague; or planning a charity run; or dwelling on an incident that happened yesterday; or wondering if you'll lose your job tomorrow.

Whatever thoughts pass through your mind – whether noble or base, flitting or devastating – don't accord them special status or offer any red-carpet treatment.

Instead, simply note their coming and note their going, just as you might note a fly on the wall or the distant sound of a passing car.

It is the start of discovering that we are neither our thoughts nor our memories, something our breathing knew long ago.

One Thing

Today, concentrate on one thing that you might not usually concentrate on. Do it or look at it or touch it or taste it for its own sake.

Perhaps you could drink a cup of coffee for its own sake, without doing anything else at the same time. It's just about the drinking and the coffee.

Perhaps, for five minutes, you could sit on the train for its own sake, without doing anything else at the same time. It's just about the sitting and the train.

Perhaps you could walk mindfully for a minute for its own sake, without concerning yourself with anything but the miracle of movement. It's just about the walking.

*Through such concentration, you gather
your fragmented self; and by touching
one thing more deeply, momentarily,
you touch life more deeply.*

Same Seed, Different Soil

Jesus told a story of the four soils.

The sower sows the seed, casting it with vigour from his bag, but it falls variously. Some seed falls on the hard path and is immediately eaten by the birds. Some falls on rocky ground and begins to grow but, without sufficient moisture, soon withers. Some falls among weeds and, on reaching a certain height, finds itself strangled by them. Some seed, however, falls on good soil and grows wonderfully.

It's a story about our ability to receive truth. The seed thrown in the good soil was exactly the same as that thrown onto the path. Yet only one batch was able to grow.

More important than the guru is our inner state. If we are good soil, we can fruitfully receive from anything. If we are poor soil, even what is good will be rejected.

To change things, it is sometimes enough to say, 'I'm poor soil today.'

On Taking Various Paths

If you take part in a pilgrimage, then you follow a single way. Pilgrims may have their own manner of walking but the path is a single way.

Pilgrims who constantly seek other paths reveal their lack of focus and a desire for escape through distraction.

'I haven't tried the other paths yet,' they say. 'They could be more interesting.'

So today they leave you to test out one path; and tomorrow they will test another. 'Have you tried this one?' they ask, already eyeing another one. 'The options are endless!'

They prefer to travel a hundred paths superficially than one path seriously.

Mindfulness is a single way, relating you
always to the present moment; though,
as to the manner of the walk, no one
will travel the path quite like you.

The Dog in the Wood

Perhaps you've heard this story... or perhaps experienced it in another guise.

The man is walking in the wood when he comes across a small dog.

He is fond of dogs and approaches it to stroke it.

Suddenly, the dog is yapping at the man, curling its lip and barking.

It's even threatening to bite!

The man steps back with an angry curse.

'Nasty piece of work,' he thinks, 'stupid dog!'

Until the realization:

The dog's back leg is caught in a trap.

The animal is snapping and barking because it's in pain.

Suddenly the man feels differently and quite forgets his cursing.

He feels only compassion for this hurting creature.

Hostility always comes from a place of pain.

So who suffers from your pain?

Opening Night

There's excitement in the theatre: the curtain is about to go up. So many people from so many places and all talking about so many things! But as the house lights dim, the chatter stops. Now there is focus, a gathering of anticipation and oneness.

And then it starts – the curtain swings back and the opening scene is revealed.

Wow!

The scene was there all the time, set up and ready, and very close to us – we just couldn't see it because of the curtain. In a similar manner, mindful awareness draws back curtains inside us, revealing what was close to us but hidden. It does this one curtain at a time; though many are drawn aside over a lifetime.

The thirteenth-century poet and mystic Rumi said this about curtains, though he called them barriers: 'Your task is not to seek love, but merely to seek and find all the barriers within yourself that you have built against it.'

When we stop the internal chatter, dim our thoughts and gather ourselves, the present scene of our lives is revealed.

The Path to This Point

Sometimes people look back on the path, which has led them to this point, and become overwhelmed by their past life. They see so much ignorance, so much stupidity and so many errors. They feel again the disgust, the disappointments and the troubles; and ask themselves... *'And all for what?'*

There is a sense that life's journey has been a detour, taking them away from what is good and hopeful and toward a wasteland of foolishness, wasted time and despair.

Yet, maybe, it has to be this way so that we can become children again, to start over again. Maybe we have to unlearn our learning; maybe we have to sleep badly in order to learn to sleep well; maybe the path must be accepted, embraced, allowed.

Whatever else has died, it isn't the small
bird of hope, singing in your chest.

Mindfulness as a Bridge

How shall we describe ourselves?

When describing human psychology, some people talk of false self and true self; others, of pretend and solid. Some find personality and essence are helpful words, while others speak of insubstantial and substantial people.

Whatever words we use to describe the human psychology, the intent is the same: we are affirming within us the existence of one land with two terrains.

The practice of mindfulness is the living and present bridge between these two terrains. We can use it to pass from false to true, from pretend to solid, from personality to essence, from insubstantial to substantial.

It is not complicated. Like any bridge, it takes us from one side to the other.

Not an Adventure Story

Some people think that the opposite of adventure is staying at home but this is not true. The opposite of adventure is self-justification.

Have you ever noticed your self-justifying self? Self-justification that furnishes you with endless escape clauses for your behaviour and presumes you have good reasons for your thoughts.

Why is this a problem?

Self-justification is insidious; while protecting us from the truth, it serves only to reveal our insecurities and deny us the adventure of truly knowing ourselves.

We're like a grand ship in a harbour, ready to sail, but with a crew too scared to head out to sea. Instead of putting up the sails and setting forth, the sailors distract themselves with arguments over who should be captain; negative comments about other boats; and self-justifying remarks like 'Do you know who you're talking to?' and 'Well, I wasn't standing for that!' and 'There's not much we don't know about sailing!'

But seasoned harbour-watchers know
that, though they love to talk of it,
they have never sailed, ever.

When and Where?

Life is an exchange between our inner and outer worlds; circumstances affect our spirit, just as spirit affects our circumstances.

It is worth noting, for instance, that Jesus, who was considered a master of prayer, rose early in the morning and walked into the hills to pray. The peace he found there was a helpful environment for his business; outer silence aided his inner silence, and this daily practice was helpful to him. After all, he would be out among the crowds soon enough.

Mindfulness can be practised in all times and places; but particular times and places help.

Prisoner's Delight

Imagine a prisoner in a cell, hemmed in and hopeless.

Imagine, then, all the confining walls disappearing suddenly, leaving the prisoner gazing into the great beyond.

Every moment of mindful attention is similarly liberating, providing freedom from the walls of our conditioned suffering: suffering that arises from our past.

The prisoner is not the walls; we are not our conditioning –

and this awareness is liberation.

The King and the Fool

The King's banquet was in full flow, when the Court Jester was summoned to perform. On arrival, he juggled for a time, played on the lute and then bowed to the King. The King toasted him with a large glass of wine.

'Thank you, your Highness,' said the Jester, 'though, as we see once again, you battle more with the wine cork than with the evils in the nation!'

Everyone in the Great Hall was suddenly quiet; but not the Jester.

'You dance excitedly with your status; and give great honour to your imaginings. But you have lost your self, and made of your beloved nation a distant and disregarded figure. You bid your people serve you! But should not you be serving them?'

The silence was deep; even the mice were hushed, as the jester continued with his tirade.

'Your Highness looks more in the mirror than he looks in his soul. But I, the jester, see the rust on your shiny crown!'

'Why do you listen to this fool?' whispered the outraged Queen in the King's ear.

'The truth doesn't flatter us,' replied the King. 'But it does free us.'

'Continue, Jester, please!'

Questions Concerning the Captain

The ship's captain is barking out orders. First he takes the boat north, and then he takes it south and then, with another order, north-west.

'North! No, south! No, north-west! D'you hear me?'

He is most clear in his commands. And, imagining that the captain knows what he's doing, the crew jump into action, as he orders the ship east, and then south-west and then north again:

'East! No, south-west! No, north!'

Each command is crisp and authoritative and can't be ignored because he is their leader.

As for the journey, the records show that so far, the ship has hit four icebergs, three fishing boats and collided with an ocean liner.

Finally, they arrive in port, damaged and four weeks late – only to discover that it's the wrong port.

'They must have moved it,' says the captain confidently.

Don't allow your thoughts to be
the captain of your ship.

Mindfulness and Freud

In Buddhist thought, enlightenment is understood not as the presence of something but as the absence of something: the permanent extinction in our lives of greed, hatred and delusion.

Enlightenment is not the acquisition of new ideas but the patient removal of old ways of being our selves. Anthony de Mello, a Jesuit priest and psychotherapist, defined truth as 'the sustained consciousness of error', which is saying the same thing. If the errors of greed, hatred and delusion are removed, only happiness remains.

Freud agreed in part. He saw people driven by two main forces – erotic drive (greed) and aggressive drive (hatred) – and acknowledged their destructive power in the human psyche.

Here the paths diverge. For while Freud regarded these forces as immovable, Buddhist psychology does not. For Freud, with such monsters at the gate, we should not expect anything more from therapy than 'ordinary human unhappiness'. In Buddhist psychology, however, these are weeds that can be uprooted.

'Ordinary human unhappiness' is not where mindfulness ends –

but where it begins.

Making Room for Happiness

I'm putting up balloons and bunting today in celebration. I've got Champagne and fireworks, too, because I want it to be the very best of welcomes.

Who's coming?

Equanimity. Yes, the rumour is that she might come to me today, hence the excitement. Imagine having the attitude of mind that can embrace both pleasure and pain, without being driven by them into desire-fuelled reaction.

Without equanimity, much of my day is coloured by grasping behaviour, which leaves no room for happiness.

What happens?

First, my behaviour becomes compulsive, like that of an animal or machine. I lose my humanity; my ability to act freely with awareness. Next, my grasping leads me to overlook the needs of others, when they conflict with my own. And last, each such act by me gives substance to a self that is nothing more than a ghostly memory of my clinging and grasping past.

So you can understand why I'm putting up the bunting, hiring the best caterers I know and spraying everything gold because, yes, equanimity is coming!

And I shall be human again.

Other People's Gardens

When prayer is desire, it can be less than holy. Some people imagine that as long as they put 'Amen' at the end, they can ask for whatever they wish. This is desire in spiritual clothes; and, whatever the nature of the desire, desire is greed.

Meister Eckhart, the thirteenth-century mystic, said that 'in true obedience, there will be no "I want this to happen" or "I want that to happen" but only a pure going out of what is our own.'

In other words, the only agent for change is who we are, and what grows out of it. So, instead of advising everyone else about his or her garden, we are asked simply to tend our own, with awareness of present experience with acceptance.

From this place, happiness flows;
and a pure going out of what is our own.

Intended Outcomes

If I were building a home to protect me from the winter, I would work hard, aware of the cold to come. I'd work with concrete, stone, wood and tile. I'd climb ladders, cement and render walls and level floors. I wouldn't notice the labour particularly, though sometimes I might be tired. I'd be thinking only of the coming winter and the intended house.

Beneath all our labour is intention. Whatever the work we do in life – and everything is work – our intention holds it, guides it and colours it. A cleaner in a hotel may feel frustrated or a film star may be depressed but their unhappiness is not caused by what they do; it is caused by the intentions they bring to what they do.

If your intention is to reach the top, it will affect how you treat people and ensure your unhappiness.

Someone asked me the other day what was my intention for the rest of my life? I was caught by surprise and, without thinking, heard myself saying, 'To face my own suffering and be kind.'

But, more importantly, what
would your answer be?

Moving Forward

If we wish to know what made us, it is best to consider psychotherapy or, perhaps, the wisdom of the Enneagram, in the company of a wise counsellor.

If, however, we wish to unmake ourselves, it is best to consider mindfulness, which can be undertaken only in our own company.

Mindfulness is ambitious. It proposes for you a wordless revolution, which seeks complete transformation of mind.

How?

Through mindfulness practice, fresh moments of insight appear to you. These fragments of clarity may remain only briefly at first, but each such moment is fuel for the next one, which may have more staying power than the last. It is slow work, but cumulative – like the warmth of the sun on a town hit by flood.

Increasingly, intuition grants us glimpses of our conditioned, constructed and changeable mental life. And from such insights and glimpses, from such wordless knowing, we know we can never go back –

only forward.

The Oft-asked Question

'What should I do?' is a common question and entirely stupid. Even those who seek a mindful way of life often want to know what they should do; or what I would do.

'What would you do?' they ask.

But these are the wrong questions.

What should I do?

What would you do?

These things are not helpful.

A more helpful question is: 'What should I *not* do?'

To which the answer is simple:

'Don't identify with your negative emotions, such as worry, suspicion, hurt, resentment and fear.'

But we ignore this helpful question; our face becomes sad, and we turn and walk away. Our psychology is rooted in another idea, which involves taking initiatives, activism and taking control. So we prefer the unhelpful question:

'What can I do?'

We ask this again and again, like one standing by a motorway, waiting for a train.

2

BECOMING
AWARE

*Ways to be aware when our
tendency is to blindness.
Opening our eyes will
reveal new things.*

What's Your Address?

A state of being is a place, yes?

Physically, most people like to live in nice homes and in a good part of town. This is their chosen place and, perhaps, they succeed in getting the right address and feel rather proud of their achievement.

But it's a meaningless address in so many ways; for their state of being is where they truly live.

If, for instance, someone's mental activity consists of resentment; or holding others to account; or feeling upset by every life event or disillusionment – then, wherever they live physically, psychologically they live in the narrowest and darkest of streets, in filth and squalor.

So if your state of being is a place, what's your address? Be mindful of this today.

Defining Moments

What defines you?

We are defined by what we want. Some say we are defined by our understanding, which is true. But the quality of our understanding arises from what we want.

Sometimes I meet people who talk of wanting to be free or wanting to be real. But they are not prepared to notice their acts and thoughts, which are stopping them from being free and real. They are happy to read about noticing; but they hold back from actually doing it. So the conclusion must be that, though they talk about it, they don't really want it.

Wanting something creates a great energy inside us, and where we channel that energy is what we become. So what do you want today? What is your aim?

If you want to become a monkey, rest assured you'll begin to resemble one.

What Are My Values?

What would you like your life to stand for?

To help you find out, why not jot down 10 words that describe you.

Friends can help you with this first stage but not after. And this first list may include positive and negative words.

Over the next 10 days, produce a new list each day – nine words, then eight words and so on until you're down to three, two... and finally, one.

The words may change as you go along. Your five words may look nothing like your original 10. Your final word may be appearing for the first time.

No negative words are allowed after day five, because ultimately they're a lie and not who you are.

Let your final words be aspirational yet truthful; rooted in your reality but with room for growth.

By day 10, your one word will speak of your core value. Wonderful!

And then just one question remains:

Are you willing openly to experience
what blocks your path there?

Lights, Camera, Action

If this was a live mindfulness show and you were the contestant in the studio, the cameras would be swinging round towards you now and the question being asked: 'What is happening right now?'

This question is the start of all mindful inquiry. Not what happened yesterday, or might happen tomorrow, but simply: what is happening inside you now?

And it's not about 'why' either. Why this is happening is a question for another time. In mindful exploration, it's just about 'what': 'What is happening right now?'

As your body becomes aware of your state, aware of what is happening, the next question is: 'Can you stay with what's happening? And can you accept what's happening? Or do you feel the urge to reject it or run away?'

Forget about the TV show;
this is much more important than that.

Young Again

If we are to make the world young again, we must ourselves become young.

We must give up playing the expert and empty ourselves of our tired knowing and false impressions.

We have become old and bent with our supposed knowledge and distorted perceptions. Our take on everything is wrong.

We don't live and learn; we live and confirm discredited patterns of understanding.

And so, if we are to make the world young again, we must ourselves become young –

and allow fresh light in the room.

Under the Bonnet

Some people drive a car with no idea how it works. This is manageable while the car is performing, but when it breaks down, there's a problem. You may be left stranded or in a panic, unsure of how to fix the problem. With no relevant resources to bring to this situation, you're in need of help. If you understood how the car worked, much of the terror would be gone. You'd know the problem and how best to deal with it. It may well be that you could sort it yourself.

Mindfulness is a science of human understanding, revealing how you work. It is a science because it involves investigation and testing; it involves looking and learning – noticing things about ourselves, which life has trained us not to see.

As I walk home from the station, I am sometimes surprised by the appearance of disturbance from nowhere. A thought appears in my head and then a strong feeling, arising from the thought, follows it. Suddenly I am snatched from my state of serenity, like one kidnapped; and I trace back the mechanics of how it happened.

Unravelling these two strands of experience – thought and feeling – reveals the restless movement of my mind, how my feelings are constructed and, as I approach home, what they do to my body.

It's like the first session of a car maintenance course.

The Boy Who Wanted to Build a Sandcastle

The boy had wanted to build a sandcastle. He told everyone that this is what he'd do on the beach that day.

'I'm going to build the best sandcastle ever!' he said, and they all looked on and clapped as he dug his spade into the sand to start.

But as the day went on and difficulties occurred, he collected beautiful shells for a while and then played exciting ball games with other children.

He enjoyed these things very much, but then started to cry, because he'd wanted above all to be a builder of sandcastles.

'Why is your sadness about the sandcastle so heavy?' asked the kind deckchair attendant, 'and the shells and the games so quickly forgotten?'

'I don't know,' said the boy. 'All I know is I feel very sad.'

Sometimes we become aware that one feeling or longing carries particular force. We can't always say why, and may cry as we allow it to pass through, and this is OK.

The Oven Door

As you will know, the oft-opened oven does not cook well.

With each opening of the door, heat is quickly lost as it pours meaninglessly into the kitchen. The focused energy of the furnace is dissipated, the intensity diminished and the high temperature distracted. The cooking inevitably suffers.

When we close the oven door, and keep it shut, we focus the heat once again and allow the oven to do what it does best.

Like the oven, every new thought is an opening of the oven door and a dissipation of our strength and focus.

As we allow our breathing to take us into our body, we watch our thoughts come and go, wasting energy; and we become more adept at closing the door of our inner space –

and guarding against half-baked notions.

Hole in the Wall Gang

When we restore something, we return it to its former state. This is the meaning of 'pristine', the way something was in the beginning.

Our sense of reality, therefore, is not in pristine condition, but barnacled and battered by our conditioning. We tend to notice only experience that serves our ongoing projects and goals.

If, for instance, I am rushing for a bus, I see only the bus, the distance between and any objects (people) in my way. I am unaware of the circling birds, a woman opening an upstairs window or a greengrocer across the road rearranging the oranges. I notice nothing, which does not relate to my goal. This leaves my sense of reality almost non-existent.

We notice those things that serve us. We welcome into our consciousness only that which helps us toward our goals or confirms our assumptions and beliefs. Everything else, we overlook.

Restoring reality involves putting distance between ourselves and our goals and beliefs. It is as though we are creating a hole in a well-defended wall, through which help can come. In the vacant space created, reality can arrive; and for no other reason than itself.

For a moment, we are in pristine condition.

How to Handle Snakes

The snake was still young and without its full quota of venom. Even so, it was causing the boy some pain.

'The snake keeps biting me!' complains the boy to his dad.

He's aware that his dad hardly ever gets bitten and yet, as a snake-handler, he handles snakes all day.

'It's all about how you hold them,' says his dad.

'How I hold them? So what should I change about the way I hold them?'

'It's helpful to hold them very lightly,' says his dad.

'But I like to grip them!'

'I know, I know. But loosen your grip and hold them ever more lightly. In that way, they won't hurt you.'

And, as with snakes, so with our theories:
we should hold them ever more lightly.

The Quality of Silence

No two silences are the same, any more than any two clouds are the same. So today, we become aware of the quality of our silence.

Perhaps we are in a hurry to be somewhere or want something to happen and our silence is impatient. Or, perhaps, our silence is a defensive and self-justifying silence, ennobling us and denouncing others. Perhaps, it is an angry silence, turbulent like a restless sea; or a numb silence unable to feel meaning.

Or perhaps it is a still silence, full of beauty and possibility, like dewy grass at the beginning of the day.

As we listen to our breathing, the quality of our silence becomes apparent. This silence determines the quality of our noise.

The Hijackers

If you're the pilot of a plane flying to London, the appearance of even one hijacker is bad news. They come to take you from your planned destination.

But what if there is not one hijacker on the plane – but a hundred?

The first stands up and tells you to fly to New York. The second insists the plane goes to Delhi. A third demands that you must land in Sydney, while a fourth will hear of no destination but Cairo. And then come all the others...

Poor plane! First it is sent in one direction, then another and then another still. You're at the controls, but not in control. The aircraft is all over the place and, after a while, with so many voices in your head, you forget your true destination.

Our thoughts act in just the same way on our day, hijacking our contentment.

Ten slow breaths, which we count in and count out, one after the other, can help remind you of who you are, why you are here and where you wish to fly.

Before, there was just one hijacking thought after another; and each one so insistent. Now, we are on the right path.

Unhelpful Projections

If you're not aware that your son is being bullied at school, you don't take the matter up with his teacher. Why would you?

And if you're not aware of cancerous cells in your body, you don't go for treatment. Again, why would you?

You can't change what you're not aware of, this is obvious; and psychologically, you're too frightened to be aware of very much.

So don't make more difficulties for yourself.

Don't, for instance, project onto others what you reject in yourself, which is what you spend much time doing. We do this out of fear, but these projections muddy the water, so you lose sight of yourself.

This is unhelpful and I think of the therapist, who projected his own lack of self-knowledge onto his clients and caused them to flounder.

Instead, bring a spirit of acknowledgement to your life, for acknowledgement feeds awareness. From here on, trace every judgement of another back to a fracture within yourself.

Instead of projecting onto others what you don't like in yourself, allow things within you; acknowledge things about yourself, without fear.

And here is peace and change.

The Value of Mud

You don't have to believe anything to be mindful; indeed, certain belief may get in the way. Worshipping an idea, however fine, soon invokes the law of diminishing returns and brings disillusionment. No single idea has arms either long enough or strong enough to hold reality.

Instead of believing anything in particular, the mindful start by taking note of their bodies and the mud of their existence.

What mud might they notice? They note their awkward breathing when scared; their tight chest when angry; the frown-locked face; the cocky swagger; the tense shoulders; the sweat of fear; the burning face of shame; the zoning out when challenged; the spiteful sneer or the furtive frightened eyes.

Some say that they have better things to do than contemplate such mud; that no good can come of it.

The Buddha wouldn't agree with them. He loved psychological mud and reckoned that noticing it was the start of wellbeing.

As he said, 'Only from mud does the beauty of the lotus flower emerge.'

Maggots and the Ballroom Beyond

When someone is in therapy, you often hear them say something like: 'I didn't know I had so many issues until I started therapy! Now I'm finding new ones that I didn't know were there!'

Heightened awareness can be similar. 'Awareness is all very well,' you might say, 'but it often appears to bring more problems than it solves.'

It's true we don't see the maggots until we lift the lid; and when we do, finding first one maggot and then beneath it another and then some more further down, it can be a bit of a shock.

But all is well, because the maggots are mere corridors to the ballroom beyond. You need the corridor; you don't need to stay there.

The Burning Boat

I remember being at Portsmouth harbour at night, and feel as though I'm there now.

There's a burning boat on the mud beach. I'm beside it but depressed, as I have been for a while. I look at the boat and think: *That's me - everything is being destroyed.* The burning boat merely reaffirms my feelings of despair.

And that's how the memory stays with me until a few years later, when someone questions my interpretation:

'Such glory in the boat's dying,' they say.

I reflect on it and suddenly see the glory. Things were dying, but there was so much glory in the dying! The wonderful orange flame in the dark night sky - stunning! Why hadn't I seen that?

I hadn't seen it because of my self-justifying self-image. I was a depressed person, a victim and everything had to be interpreted through this bleak prism. A burning boat! Well, that had to be negative - cue more despair.

Left in this state, I would have justified myself to hell, which is where a lot of us are for much of the time, defending our soiled perceptions.

I sometimes ask people: 'What is it that you're defending here?' More often than not, they're defending nothing nobler than their right to unhappiness.

The Seventh Sense

Can you see the six doors? They're worth watching.

These are the six doors of our senses – sight, smell, taste, touch, hearing and thought – through which human experience arrives.

Experience is pushing at each door, even as you read. Through the doors of touch, sight and thought, you experience the pages of this book and the words on the page; while through the door of smell, you experience, perhaps, your clean clothes.

Through the door of taste, you might experience the sweetness of a biscuit, while through hearing, you experience the traffic outside. There's so much arriving through the doors.

And now watch again, because something important is happening. Greeting each new arrival is a feeling, which sets the tone of your response.

Feeling is the seventh sense and a powerful one. Our feelings act like an overbearing butler with a weak master. Feeling not only greets each of my six senses, it then defines how I react to them; how I construct my moment.

Our seventh sense of feeling, like the butler, needs watching; he, perhaps, assumes too much power.

Salt in the Wound

Salt sprinkled on healthy skin isn't a problem. It is easily brushed off, if noticed at all. After all, our body produces salt when we exercise so it is not an enemy.

If you have a flesh wound, however, then salt brings pain and reaction. 'It's rubbing salt in the wound' as the saying goes. But it's the wound, and not the salt, which is sparking the reaction.

This is true also of psychological pain so, today, we'll be aware of when it appears and why. When something or someone acts like salt, we'll react only if we carry a wound.

Our failing is not to be wounded; our failing is to ignore the wound while attacking everyone else in pained reaction. These people don't need our attention; but our wounded places do.

Which wound in me created that reaction? And what caused the wound?

These are the questions.

The Engagement

The boy's mother was getting ever more frustrated with her son, Silvio. His behaviour was becoming increasingly ridiculous.

'I've just got engaged, Mother!' he said. 'Isn't it wonderful?'

'You got engaged to someone else yesterday.'

'I did, yes, but this is different.'

'And Silvio, have you forgotten you got engaged twice last Sunday?'

'I know, I know and they were both dear people.'

'I've lost count of your engagements.'

'That's possible, Mother, but this one's the girl of my dreams! I just know she's Miss Right.'

'So were the others, Silvio; you were passionate about them all.'

'This time it's really real.'

'Until the next one! You don't have to get engaged every time you meet a girl. You could just have a coffee.'

Watching thoughts come and go, without engaging with them, frees us from brooding. This is the thing: we don't have to get engaged.

A Question over Coffee

There is a cost, if that is the right word.

When conscious – aware of our present experience with acceptance – then you won't be less aware of the pain of others; you will be more aware.

The other day I had coffee with a man in a shopping mall and, though we talked of a number of things, only one question pressed itself upon me. And so I asked him:

'What does anger feel like in your body?'

'It's probably time I faced it,' he said in a matter-of-fact way, as though we'd discussed it at length, though neither of us had spoken of it before.

It is good to be part of a circle, where the awareness of one person nudges awareness in another and so on.

A Cautionary Tale

Here's a strange thing:

She has the largest collection of all-promising, all-healing self-help books that I know of; yet in my experience, she is a woman least able to receive the truth.

She makes exciting plans for her super-spiritual search, while daily she pushes away unwanted realities. 'These are nothing to do with my search!' she declares. 'I seek to move onto a higher plain!'

This woman likes nothing better than to read about awareness; though she lacks the courage to experience it for herself, now.

As a walking book of helpful spiritual quotations, she seems to know everything, yet understands nothing.

When the truth leaves her head and enters her being, filling its corridors like a sweet aroma, this will be a good day.

The Hardest Word?

In the supermarket where I used to work, we weren't allowed to say sorry to customers.

'Don't say sorry!' we were told.

The store was happy to refund you for the dented can of beans or exchange the tart oranges for sweeter ones. But you never got a 'Sorry'.

'It isn't the message we want to give,' we were told.

'So what is the message we want to give?' I asked.

'We need to be positive, Simon. This is a competitive industry. People must leave the store feeling they're part of a success story!'

This is why, on the shop floor, we were also forbidden from using the word 'unfortunately'. It wasn't deemed positive enough; it had the slight whiff of failure.

In this matter, the supermarket displayed the stupidity of the insecure.

I am not diminished by saying sorry... I am freed.

Apology doesn't break relationships;
it liberates them.

My Intentions, Honourable or Otherwise

I will notice my intentions today; the attitude I assume toward something that is happening.

Some people think there is nothing we can do about our intentions; that they are somehow written in stone: 'That's just the kind of guy I am!'

But intentions are choices I make, minute by minute as life arises around me and within me. How will I deal with this situation? Whether at home or at work, intention determines what I'm going to do about it.

So what will be my intention now? Shall I embrace what is happening or resist it, because the two are not the same. Or again, do I prolong this conversation or do I terminate it? Shall I take out my frustration on this person or not? With the facts before me, will I be cold or encouraging? Shall I be passive and slow down to irritate others or actively help? Intentions can be carried out in a wordless fashion.

Whether on the phone or on the bus, I will notice my intentions today. And I will notice the dispositions that inform my intentions, which – like over-eager advisors to the President – can end up making policy on the hoof.

My intentions may or may not be honourable;
but they will be noticed.

Thoughts of God

If God fills your thoughts, you may be in trouble; for when your thoughts end, so will your God.

Thoughts are the most changeable things and, if they are to carry our God, it is like leaving a drunk in charge of a baby.

A God of thoughts is quickly ill. When our thoughts harden, so will our God; and when our thoughts are distracted, so is our God. And a hard God or a distracted God is a God who looks rather like you.

If God is our journey, we need a God that is beyond thought and imaginings, who inhabits our heart and being; a God who we see happily in all things; who leaves us unencumbered by attachments and with a free mind.

Perhaps free minds are one of the clearest signs of God's presence; minds liberated from preference.

Beware of Love

It may be a strange thing to say but beware of love today, wherever you come across it, whether it is in the newspapers, a magazine article or in conversation.

The word 'love' generally describes an emotion, which emerges inside us via highly toxic channels. In current understanding, it is a feeling gripped by possessiveness, chaperoned by jealousy and with its alter ego, hate, waiting ready in the wings.

Love such as this – whether parental, amorous or social – is an emotion, which is genuinely short on charm: easily upset, manipulative and, even, vindictive.

The enlightened have no relationship with this emotion, preferring instead the pure feeling of compassion, which, unlike love, does not flow through the polluting channels of the ego.

And this is why it is so charming.

The Man Who Wanted Shoes

See the poor man who wanted a pair of shoes. This man desired shoes, longed for them above all else.

His longing was so well known in the community that a kind benefactor gave him the leather he needed. But he had to make the shoes himself, so they truly fitted him.

This meant that the poor man had to wait a little longer for his shoes, which he grumbled about to begin with, but soon came to appreciate.

The benefactor could have given him a pair of his shoes but this wouldn't have worked. The poor man must have his own shoes and not those borrowed from another.

We may long to be aware but we can't borrow someone else's awareness. We can use their teaching – but our awareness must be made from our own lives.

3

BECOMING
PRESENT

*Ways to be present, when our
tendency is to be absent;
and why we are happier and
healthier living in the moment.*

Breath of Life

Breathing exercises are a simple and profound way into mindfulness because they gift us with the present. Wherever our thoughts or emotions may be taking us, backward or forward in time, our breathing is refreshingly present and invites us to join it there.

You could notice your breathing now. As you count each breath in and each breath out, you are inwardly strengthened, simply by the return of your being to the present. The present is nourishing because it's where you're meant to be; it's like putting a plant in sunlight.

As you breathe in and out, distractions will appear; one thought after another will try to snatch you from the present. Note each distraction kindly, however many there are; and return each time to your breathing; to being present, to being strengthened –

to being conscious.

Entering the Fire

Three young men, Shadrach, Meshach and Abednego, were thrown into the fire. The men had refused to worship the Babylonian king Nebuchadnezzar II and, in preparation for their deaths, the furnace had been made seven times hotter than usual.

The soldiers, who threw them into the furnace, were badly scalded, yet the three men were quite unharmed by the flames; and Nebuchadnezzar was disturbed to see what looked like a fourth figure in the furnace with them. Was it a guardian angel?

This story is told in the book of Daniel in the Old Testament and reminds us that the present can appear like a furnace: a furnace of truth that we avoid when we worship at the shrine of endless distraction.

No harm came to Shadrach, Meshach and Abednego and, like them, we need fear nothing. The present has its own guardian angel.

The Hard Edge

There needs to be a hard edge to our intentions or they are nothing.

I'm teaching myself the piano, I'd like to play well.

But the hard edge is this: I need to practice to be better.

I set myself 10 minutes a day, which isn't much but does mean I do it.

It's a possible target.

So what do you intend for your life?

And what do you propose to do about it? Where's the hard edge of authenticity?

It's worth a thought.

There needs to be a hard edge to our intentions... or they are nothing.

Meditation of Attention

The meditation of attention is a simple practice and one that you can do anywhere, at any time of day. It can be done as easily on a bus as in a temple and only takes a few minutes.

In this meditation, we intentionally focus our attention on one thing, as opposed to many things; and return our attention to the present.

It doesn't matter what you focus on, because the world is your friend, and will speak freely with you, whether you work on a farm, an oilrig or in an office.

What you choose to focus on is up to you: whether it's an object in your home or one seen on your daily travels; whether it's something beautiful, odd or entirely commonplace and unremarkable – you are invited to consider it.

Become aware of its appearance, its setting and its composition. Who and what has gone into its making? And what is its role now? Will it last many years or only briefly? How does it feel? What else does it silently say to you?

No aspect of the world is silent
when given present attention.

Watching the Clock

I have a new clock, which stops me going mad; and it makes me wonder if these clocks shouldn't be more widely available – to stop other people going mad.

It's a normal clock in many ways. It's circular, in traditional fashion, and boasts an hour hand, minute hand and second hand, all of which click happily around the clock's face.

But for someone like myself – who can spend too much time imagining future scenes that don't exist, and getting angry, fearful or anxious about them – the new clock is wonderful.

Its distinguishing feature is that there aren't any numerals on its face; there isn't a circle of one to twelve. Instead, where each number should be, in various colours, is just the word *Now*.

What time is it? *Now*. In fact, on my clock, it's only ever now, which suits me well.

I'm so much happier in the present, where all is perfect.

How Will I Know?

How will I know when I am present?

In the present, I will have no enemies to hold to account, no vendettas to plot and no disappointments on which to brood.

Animosity and disappointment are too obese with undigested history to exist in the present; they can't get through the door.

So here we are in the present – free of either judgement or resentment.

*How delightful it is for our body to be
lifted clear from that lake of toxic waste.*

The Present Moment

In the *Gospel of Thomas*, the followers of Jesus said: 'Tell us who you are, so that we may believe in you.'

Like us, they were busy searching for meaning.

Jesus answers them: 'You search the face of heaven and earth, but you do not recognize the one who is in your presence; and you do not know how to experience the present moment.'

We're not the first to be so busy searching
that we miss the meaning of now.

Energy for Life

Mindfulness is not a good idea. It is much better than that.

Mindfulness is energy for touching life more deeply, more kindly, more safely and more insightfully.

This energy, which we call forth from ourselves, brings us to mindful sitting, walking or standing.

Here, we breathe in our suffering or our excitement or our restlessness, and in time, truth becomes apparent; a way becomes apparent because there is always a way.

Our mindful energy brings us into the present. The present then greets us, crashes through us like a waterfall and generates the energy of fresh experience, arising from unknown places within us.

Melting Time

In linear time, everything has to be moving toward something, developing into something else. We like to think of our lives as progressing, as a journey we're on, making our way forward towards some future time.

But progress lies not in the passage of time but in our understanding of time. For past, present and future all exist as one in the eternal present. The seed contains the flower; the newborn baby is also the old man; the despairing soul is also the joyful soul. Yes, the darkness is the light and the selfish person the saint. Everything in this moment contains all other things.

We use mental images to create a time to come, because our thinking is linear and separating, and only understands one thing after another. But, in contemplation, there is no time but now, in which all that was, is and will be exist simultaneously. So no time is held to be better or worse, for each moment is complete in itself, fulfilled in itself and the whole truth, from beginning to end.

In this way, we progress towards nothing, because we're already there.

Beyond the
Puppet House

Ray the puppet maker is asked by his colleague Barney if he wishes to come out for a drink tonight.

'No thank you,' replies Ray.

'Why not?' says Barney.

'I'm going to spend the evening in the company of my puppets.'

'But you always do this,' says Barney.

'I know.'

'They're not real people!'

'They're what I want them to be,' says Ray, 'and that's good enough for me.'

'And then you'll go home, I suppose?'

'No. I'm spending the night in the puppet house I made.'

'But it's make-believe!'

'It's just how I want it.'

'But you have a real home out there!'

At which point Ray throws a blanket over his head, and says that he can't see Barney's point at all.

It has been said that the world is only as real as I am. So my practice today, as I become present, is to allow scenes and people to be real, unmade and un-invented by me.

Noticing the Sausage Machine

Only a fool would be surprised when the shape of a sausage appears from a sausage machine. After all, that is the shape and form of the machine: tubular and squeezy. What else could appear but a sausage?

In like manner, our present comes shaped by our past. And what shape can the past create other than itself? So although our moments pretend to be fresh, they come to us stale – musty with the smell of old perceptions, feelings and intentions.

Mindful meditation, however, creates only fresh moments; moments infused with energies conjured from the eternal present, which makes all things new.

Today, we'll notice the sausage machine of old reaction; and, when we can, turn off the power.

The Bathroom Floor Is Enough

I was on my knees yesterday, cleaning the bathroom floor, when I found myself thinking that I might be able to do the kitchen as well, if I hurried. So I began to hurry, cleaning in haste, which caused me to knock my arm against the side of the bath.

Ouch!

Fortunately, then I recovered consciousness and stopped hallucinating about the kitchen. I let go of hurry and distraction, and returned to the present and the bathroom floor - noticing the pattern on the floor tiles for the first time.

It was both a joy and a relief to be home.

Warm Currents

When swimming in the cold sea, we sometimes find a warm current enveloping our legs beneath the surface. It's a sweet discovery and brings warmth to our chilly bodies.

The warmth is an elusive friend, however, for it's lost in the swirling depths as quickly as it was found. So we move our bodies to find it again, adjusting ourselves beneath the surface, stretching out a leg to enjoy the warm place again.

In the same way, we return our selves to the present: making adjustments beneath the surface to find the elusive warmth again.

Like a Panther

As we settle into our breathing and into the present, we note any concerns, which take us from the present.

Perhaps they are concerns, which take us back into the past, as we return to someone's words or a particular event. Or perhaps they take us into the future, as we anticipate a conversation or an outcome – happy or frightening.

We are constantly taken from the present by our multiple lives. It's like a person who tries to sit still, and then scratches an itch in one place and then another and then another. They end up doing everything but sitting still.

Yet, as we allow our multiple thoughts to come and go, we begin to touch our substance.

From multiplicity to simplicity; from scattered to collected; from distraction to focus –

like a panther gathering itself to leap.

Our Substantial Self

Have you ever felt you've lost something along the way? Lost touch with something strong and beautiful inside?

It's a common feeling because, of course, we have.

In order to survive, we had to say goodbye to our truest self. We've had to chisel a personality that can make its way in the world, but isn't who we are.

It helped us survive, which is good... but it can't give us happiness.

So what now?

Julian of Norwich, the fourteenth-century contemplative, was the first English woman to write a book; and in it, she speaks of our substantial and insubstantial self.

The brave are becoming what they truly are, their more substantial selves.

The less brave are staying with their old personality, their insubstantial self.

I suspect you are one of the brave.

Keep Talking

Mindfulness may land us in a jungle.

While psychological theories provide a map of our inner jungle, mindfulness drops us right in the middle of it; and this can, on occasion, be frightening.

It has to be this way. The experience of the jungle must be our own; no one can walk it for us. We'll be wise, however, if we find a companion on our journey, with whom we can talk about what we find.

Why is this wise? If awareness of the present brings awareness of pain, we'll feel alone, which is not helpful. As children, it was when we felt left alone that we left our true selves; and the experience of loneliness may encourage us to run away again now.

And so it's good to keep talking. As we journey back to our essence, it's good to remind ourselves that we are not alone. Often I get emails saying: 'I had to tell someone!'

And it's true, we do.

I Desire Anxiety

Do you know an anxious person or are you one yourself?

Then you'll be aware that an anxious person is never made better by having their anxiety sorted, for then another appears. Anxious soil creates a crop of anxieties, regardless of circumstance. Cut one down and up pops another; as one problem is sorted, another is already in view.

It's the same with desire. If one desire is fed, another hungry desire presents itself; and as one is put to bed, another one wakes up. In this way, our life becomes a sad stagger from one 'if only' to another – a state which removes any sense of meaningful or lasting peace.

Anxiety is a particular sort of desire; it is the desire for distraction away from the present. The self fears exposure to the present and so desires the focus to be distracted by some past or future worry.

In taking us from the present, anxiety
takes us from the only place on
Earth where all is quite well.

The Man Who Loved Medical Books

Melvyn loved medical books. Nothing gave him greater pleasure than to peruse medical dictionaries, in order to find out what was wrong with him.

Melvyn hadn't any need of doctors; instead, he had the printed word and the clear conclusions he drew from self-diagnosis. And what could be a more foolproof way to proceed?

And Melvyn lived an interesting life until the age of 39, when he died of a misprint.

Like our amateur medic, we display an infatuation with our theories, which we construct from a few scraps of evidence. Once in place, all the information is organized to fit with them; and what doesn't fit is ignored. As Abraham Maslow said, 'If you only have a hammer, you tend to see every problem as a nail.'

How can mindfulness help us in our addiction to theory?

The simple practice of present breathing immediately creates distance between my self and my thoughts. In the present, I don't know what the future holds, whereas my theories have much to say about it.

Our theories exist to give us the illusion of control. Rooted in the present, we know that we have none, and that's OK.

The Mad Elephant

It is understood that we have three centres of operation inside us. These are comprised of our intellectual centre, which is concerned with our thoughts; our moving centre, which is concerned with our will and our bodies; and our emotional centre, which is concerned with our feelings. The three centres are intimately related, as all things are.

The emotional centre is the hardest to handle, as it is the hardest to separate from. If we take our emotional state for granted, as though it is inevitable and outside our jurisdiction, it can acquire the power of a rampaging elephant, dangerous and out of control.

Mindfulness brings two tamer elephants alongside the mad one, either side of it – the intellectual centre and the moving centre. Perhaps, we use our mind to focus on the present and put things in perspective. Perhaps, we use our still bodies to inhale calm and exhale panic.

With such companions, the mad elephant of emotional response is led into the peaceful present.

Home Truths

Perhaps, mindfulness is hardest in the home. Home is where deep-rooted patterns of behaviour have established themselves, and where our reactions are habitual, automatic and often emotionally charged.

Bringing awareness of the present moment into our home life is challenging and refreshing. We begin to notice what we are feeling, moment by moment, and the everyday occurrences and exchanges that cause us to behave in a certain way. This heightened awareness of our behaviour and reactions might bring new discoveries.

And even as we are noticing these things, we are placing a holy pause in proceedings before our habitual reactions kick in.

One helpful act is to pause at the door of your home before entering. Whatever you have come from, and whatever faces you now, become a clear space for a moment, before turning the key; and then take your mindful self inside.

There is now the possibility that we might respond rather than react –

because the present has no history.

No Turning Back

In the book of Genesis, Lot and his family leave their home, the doomed city of Sodom. Famously, against advice, Lot's wife looks back for a moment and is turned into a pillar of salt.

And the truth of this fable echoes across the centuries.

There remains in our conditioned selves a great energy for looking back; for regressing; for returning to old patterns.

We reach a place in our lives where nothing much is happening, or perhaps things are happening, which makes us panic. Maybe it is a place of darkness and unknowing, and our reaction is to cast lingering looks behind us; to turn back into what we once were or return to old ways and old formulations.

But just as there was no return for those leaving Sodom, there is no return to our former selves for us. How could there be? We would return only to a dried-out husk and live there as a stranger.

We are becoming; and there is no turning back.

Advice When Kidnapped

Sometimes it happens; sometimes we are dragged from our home by worry, rage, fear, depression or desire.

We are grabbed violently, told it's not worth struggling, drugged up, hauled outside, driven away before being thrown out of the van and left miles from home, wandering and lost.

Whether it's been hours, days, weeks or years, it is our breathing that can return us home; for no kidnap can survive sustained exposure to the present.

And our breathing knows no other place to be.

Virgins Again

The call is to become virgins again, which is less foolish than it sounds.

Like a stained teacup, layered with residue, we are stained with alien images, which each leave their mark on our psyche. Each image obscures reality in some way and prompts us to react in mechanical fashion.

'That may be true,' you say. 'But how can we possibly be free of images? The world is full of them; we'd have to leave the world to escape their presence!'

And that is exactly what we do when we become present; we leave the world. Images exist in our memory, but there is no memory in the present and so there are no images staking their claim.

In this life, we can never say a complete goodbye to images; we live with their presence. But we can say goodbye to their power, as in the present moment, we are free and empty and quite unattached.

In the present, we are virgins again.

Mighty Oaks

It is a sobering thought that life does not automatically result in self-development. Many people imagine that, as they get older, they develop but this is far from inevitable. The passage of time does not make for growth.

Think of a seed. Like us, a seed is genetically programmed to grow into a plant; but it will stay a seed for a million years unless conditions for growth are right. The seed is crammed full with potential; but it won't change until placed in the soil and fed with food, air and light.

And so it is with humans. We are self-developing organisms, but life does not develop us if it's not the right sort of life.

The human being is no more the finished article than the acorn. In order to become an oak tree, the acorn needs to be planted in something other than itself, and we are the same.

Present awareness with acceptance is good soil.

Negative Capability

The English Romantic poet Keats called living in the present moment 'negative capability', and believed it essential in any who wished to be creative.

He described negative capability as the state 'of being in uncertainties, mysteries, doubts without any irritable reaching after fact or reason'.

This definition brings us to the doorstep of mindfulness. Keats describes a space within humans, which is beyond traditional certainties and can be inhabited without panic.

Here is an inner space, beyond organizing words, which seeks a different knowing, a more immediate understanding of human experience. After all, an understanding acquired at the hands of others is no understanding at all.

For the sake of his art, therefore, Keats was willing to let go of one way, in order to find another. And as our breathing brings us into the present, where there are no certainties, we do the same –

and discover a different sort of knowing, 'without any irritable reaching after fact or reason'.

Stormy Seas

Sadness and anger are closely related. Both are concerned with loss and longing, past and future. They come, when allowed, with devastating power.

It is good to allow them; but it is dangerous to be drowned by them. Like a stormy sea, they can frighten us with their turbulent power and crashing waves.

If you fear drowning, stay with your breathing, because stronger than the loss and longing is the fragile now.

Like a lighthouse along the rocky coast, mindful breathing can guide you to a safe harbour through the crashing water and battering winds.

A Five-Year Plan?

Every company has a business plan.

'This is where we want to be in five years' time,' they say.

But what's that worth when the future doesn't exist?

We can speculate about possible future scenarios.

But we can neither plan for them all nor even guess at them all; for much of life appears from nowhere.

We can respond presently to events... but we cannot predict them.

We'll be fine... as long as we remember plans can be held no more firmly than smoke.

We can pretend to plan... and laugh a little as we do.

And perhaps one day, a company will say:

'Where do we want to be in five years' time?
Present, as we are now.'

4

BECOMING
TRUST

Ways to acceptance,
when our tendency is rejection.
Trust makes all the difference.

The Supermarket Queue

Mindfulness starts at the supermarket checkout, where our queue is sure to be going slower than the one next to us. This is good training ground for surrender; and surrender is best started in small ways.

Once we have surrendered to the moment in the checkout queue, things improve. We begin to notice those around us, who were previously just a blurred background to our irritation. We also notice how happy we are, having accepted our circumstances, and brought ourselves into the aware present. Our happiness may well lead us to reach out to others with a smile or cheery remark.

And here's another beneficial thing about mindfulness. When you realize you've forgotten the beans, relations with those around you are so good that the person behind is happy to hold your place while you nip back and get them.

It's all going very well.

A Strange Solidarity

Mindfulness meditation is the art of fearless detection; the clues are in our present experience.

Perhaps you wake at night, troubled. It takes you a moment to realize that unresolved feelings have disturbed you. Becoming aware of this, you focus on your breathing, with an enquiring spirit. What is happening now? How is the trouble revealing itself in my body and mind?

You may be tempted to leave the scene and escape the investigation, by opting for a secondary pursuit, like turning on the telly or reading for a while. If, however, you're able to stay with the feeling, you can use your breath to become present.

It may be that you now recognize the source of this inner disturbance; an anger, perhaps, or sadness or fear. Whatever it is, you are simply breathing with what is happening, almost in solidarity.

You are allowing the feeling and breathing with it. It has only woken you because it thought it wasn't allowed...

A Peace of Truth

Mindfulness is not a peace comprised of lies; a peace that survives only because we turn away from unwanted energies inside us. Rather, it's a peace comprised of truth, which invites us to turn away from nothing and to accept everything.

So I don't chase away unwelcome energies when I sense their presence in me. Like bored teenagers, chasing them away only excites them. And these energies bring both a message from the past and a truth about my present.

So whether it's hate, envy, rage, fear or despair, whatever forms the turbulence takes, I don't reject but accept.

As I breathe in, I accept the distorted energy; and as I breathe out, I wish it well. Breathe in acceptance, breathe out good wishes.

And like bored teenagers, once accepted,
turbulence finds new ways of being.

'I Don't Judge Others'

A woman came to see me. She was called Valerie and she told me that, though she judged herself, she didn't judge others.

The matter had arisen because my experience of Valerie that afternoon had been one of judgement, repeated and harsh.

'I feel you are judging me,' I told her, 'and in attributing bad motives to me, you make me feel devalued as a person.'

'Oh, I'm not judging you,' she replied. 'I judge myself but I don't judge others.'

What we do to ourselves, however, we pass on to others, as sure as summer follows spring. Much of Valerie's suffering stems from her present inability to accept herself as someone who judges others. Refusing to acknowledge this person, refusing to accept them, she struggles on with her cover story.

> *It's a good day when we're courageous enough to accept ourselves as we truly are; it is like sunshine after the rain.*

When Self-Help Books Don't Help

Reading the restaurant menu is not the same as eating their food.

And reading self-help books is not the same as awareness.

A staircase exists to take you somewhere else. And when you are there, you don't stay on the stairs, but step off.

Their task is done.

And so it is with spiritual reading. It only exists to take you to yourself.

And when there, you put it aside to engage with whatever is arising in you.

Other people's words can only get in the way now.

It's time to leave the stranger on the stairs.

An Angel Is Not Enough

Suddenly there is an angel in her room, but what will be the outcome?

Nothing was certain in the story of Jesus' birth. The appearance of the angel Gabriel to Mary may have frightened her, but it didn't settle anything. They could have talked for hours without anything changing. Indeed, we often use words to distract ourselves from the present.

Nothing could happen until Mary gave her consent. It was only when she gave up her will and left her self, that new space was created within her: space that was filled with new life, with Jesus.

'Let it be to me according to your word,' she said, in an attitude of acceptance and abandonment.

Accepting that which is, and abandoning
our will, creates fertile space.

The Incident with the Tricycle

Henry, a little boy in the nursery, was riding his tricycle, when three other boys stopped him. They put their feet on the wheel, and said they wanted it. Henry was upset, but didn't know what to do with his feelings.

At this point, one of the nursery workers intervened. She asked Henry if he wanted to say anything to the three boys. He said he wasn't sure, so the nursery worker said she'd stay there while he told the boys what he felt. Strengthened by her presence, he said, 'I don't like what you're doing to me. It makes me unhappy.'

Trusting the presence of the nursery worker, Henry was able to give voice to his feelings in the moment and resolve his unhappiness. Without her help, his present feelings would have been buried in an unmarked grave and rotted there, unacknowledged.

It is helpful to take less notice of our opinions and more notice of our feelings; especially the ones we've buried, because we didn't know what to do with them.

Streak of Light

Today, I saw the dawn break through a gap in the curtains. They were heavy curtains, covering most of the large window, but they didn't quite join; and there, through the gap, was a thin sliver of brightening sky and the outline of trees, clear silhouettes against the strengthening light.

I could see very little, for the gap in the curtains was small; but I could see enough to know that darkness was done.

Today, when we find ourselves closed in by life, when the curtains of circumstance seem heavy, trust that an opening remains through which daybreak shines –

reassuring us that all is well.

The Golden Thread

Whatever we do for someone –
even if we were to die a thousand times for them –
we cannot take the slightest part of their destiny on
ourselves.

We'd best let them take their course,
just as we have taken ours, to stand where we are
now.

It's hard to let others be; hard to let go of another's
destiny.
But the same golden thread, which draws you on
through a thousand and one experiences,
draws them on also –

through a thousand and one
different experiences.

Jumping into the Sea

Everyone wants awareness, while, at the same time, wishing that his or her life were different. Unfortunately, this is like wanting to keep dry while jumping into the sea.

Awareness can't arise if we are always saying 'if only'; if we are wishing our experience to be different from how it is now.

If we say 'If only this could happen', or 'If only that were not so', we momentarily leave the present for the knotted imaginings of our self. And how can awareness possibly escape when bound by these tangled cords?

We all want awareness, while wishing our life was different, but this can't be.

If we accept our present experience, and make our home in the moment, then we undo the knots, cut the ropes

and become awareness.

On the Other Side of Anxiety

Beyond anxiety is the acceptance of anxiety, which is the greater gain.

Let's watch the process.

We feel a fear or sense rising panic and accept the arrival of this uncomfortable reaction. It's a physical sign of life that we're learning to accept our body and mind as they are, rather than how we want them to be. We understand that we only deepen suffering by trying to avoid it. The appearance of anxiety is a setback, yet fighting it is worse.

And so it is that beyond anxiety is not the absence of anxiety, but an increasing capacity to accept it as a visitor.

It isn't who you are, though it likes to give you that impression. Neither does it live with you, so you don't have to struggle with it in endless dispute. It is a visitor, always a visitor, and will leave of its own accord, as one who passes through.

As the Swedish say, 'Thank you for coming, thank you for going.'

Not Wishing, but Living

In Hermann Hesse's book *Siddhartha*, the lead character, now an old man, reflects on his life. Over the years, he has been many things and feels he has wandered often from the right path.

After much reflection, however, he comes to the conclusion that he needed to fall short; that he needed his lust, vanity, materialism and terrible despair.

Why?

'In order to give up all resistance,' explains Siddhartha, 'in order to learn how to love the world, in order to stop comparing it to some world I wished, I imagined, some kind of perfection I had made up –

but to leave it as it is and to love it and to enjoy being a part of it.'

Revelation on the Hill

I was sitting on the bus, watching a small child trying to talk to his father. The boy was full of observations and questions. His father was trying to read his book, however, and only grunted replies.

In the end, his frustration at being disturbed by the child got the better of him: 'Just give your mouth a rest, all right!' he barked. The boy sat in silence, like a flower cut down.

I was angry at the man's treatment of his son, until on reflection, I could see similar traits in myself. And now I was just sad – sad at the routine and common-place murder of hope in the world.

I battled with this idea, as the bus trundled on, finding no peace until, on the brow of the hill, I accepted this sad truth. Instead of thinking restlessly about it, I received the painful truth inside me.

Once done, something in me was able to relax and, for the first time, I experienced the possibility of good outcomes. Pain changes in colour and consistency on being accepted.

I smiled at the boy as he left.
He smiled back and waved his little hand.

'I Just Want to Feel Better!'

'So what do you want to do with yourself?' asks the therapist.

'Do with myself? I just want to feel better,' says the young man.

'Maybe,' says the therapist, 'but that isn't what I asked.'

'Look, I just want to feel better, all right? That's your job, isn't it? To make that happen.'

'OK. So tell me, what relationship do you have with your pain?'

'What relationship do I have with my pain? I haven't come here to talk about pain! I want to talk about getting better.'

'Yes. And I don't think I can help you.'

'But you're supposed to have compassion for me!'

'You need compassion for yourself first; compassion for your pain-filled self. While you ignore him and reject him, there's not much to be done.'

'But I just want to feel better!'

Mindfulness offers present and accepting space; not all are able to step into it.

Dreams of Moscow

If I long to be in Moscow, then I can't live happily in New York. An obsession with Moscow will mean that I struggle to experience New York, for much of me isn't there.

It's also true that awareness can't arise in us if we wish our experience to be other than it is. Does this make sense?

If we are living in New York, but longing to be in Moscow, we are distracted, which literally means 'ripped apart'.

Awareness arises as we allow ourselves to be where we are, who we are and how we are – with acceptance.

Who knows? I may move to Moscow
one day – next week, next year?

This is possible. But presently, I accept New York, which is quite perfect for me now.

Good News

I received some very good news this morning. I discovered that I'm full of spite towards various people.

Wonderful!

It is not the spite that is the good news, but the fact that I've allowed myself to notice it, instead of dressing it up as something else, like moral outrage or justified contempt.

I don't accept that my spite is helpful; but I do accept the truth of my spiteful state. This is how I am today.

How are you today?

A Mindful Habitat

If Seth the cameraman wants to get a glimpse of the little-known gold-crested marsh warbler he'll need to create the right conditions.

This is why he parks his car away from the scene and ensures that none of his noisy colleagues are nearby; then he stays very still in the long grass.

Long experience teaches him that if the gold-crested marsh warbler is at all suspicious or fearful, it will never appear. And, of course, Seth is interested in the gold-crested marsh warbler only, and not in other birds that might appear similar.

Likewise, if we want to get a glimpse of our little-known feelings, the right conditions are a spirit of acknowledgement; a spirit that won't judge or reject any emotions that reveal themselves to us.

If the gold-crested marsh warbler senses danger in the air, it never appears.

'Don't Pass My Glasses'

If we're given glasses inappropriate for our eyes, it's hard to see. We'll have impaired vision and probably develop a headache. In this state, we'll neither view the world clearly nor feel well disposed towards it.

It is the same with desire. Seeing the world through the lens of desire, we miss a great deal. We are so absorbed with what we want and what's best for ourselves that we see little else. With the view cluttered by personal agendas, it is like looking at a beautiful room through a dirty keyhole.

In this state, we are constantly hurt, angered or disappointed by events, which don't suit us. Everything feels personal, like an attack on 'me'.

So, today, notice when you wear these glasses and remove them. What will happen?

You will see the whole world rather than just a distracted fraction. The headache of offence lifts wonderfully when you release your claims on the moment and accept what is, without pre-condition.

Those glasses never suited you anyway.

Not My Will

'Lord, give me only what you will, and in the way that you will.'

This is how you should pray, says Meister Eckhart, 'not with many requests but with the attitude of acceptance.'

He goes on to compare these two forms of prayer. He says the latter 'is as far above the former, as heaven is above earth. And just as true obedience should have no "I want this" in it, neither should it have "I don't want," either; for "I don't want" is "pure poison for all true obedience".'

I'm now reminded of Jesus is in the Garden of Gethsemane, shortly before he is arrested and crucified. He senses that death awaits him and, like most people, he doesn't wish to die. He's aware of how he feels, aware of present experience, but also accepting: 'Not my will, but Your will be done,' he prays.

Such acceptance is not always easy. We are told Jesus sweated drops of blood in Gethsemane.

Secrets of Self-healing

Whatever feelings emerge from mindful breathing, we won't stick a judgement on them.

We might feel alone; we might feel excited; we might feel guilty, mean-spirited, murderous even, or perhaps joyful, envious, peaceful, angry, compassionate or sad. Who knows?

Whatever we feel, it is good news, because the truth is always good news when the alternative is pretence.

What matters is not so much the feeling itself, as this will pass, but that we acknowledge the feeling.

Those who are courageous enough
to acknowledge what they feel
become self-healing organisms.

Warmth on a Cold Walk

The wind was cold today,
and though dressed with protecting layers,
the chill chased me, pushed me,
penetrating to my skin,
as I hunched my shoulders to proceed along the
river path.

And I might have turned back on my walk,
this was my thought,
until the sun smiled,
cracking the clouds, all golden warmth,
holding and surprising;
and shoulders now un-hunch as I proceed along
the river.

The sun amidst the cold,
and that made all the difference.

Acceptance Questioned

Mindfulness invites us to accept our present situation. But what if our situation is crushing us? How can the hostage not wish to be free or the prisoner released?

The mystic St John of the Cross wrote of great things in prison, but he still took the opportunity to escape when he could. (He tied sheets together and climbed out the window.)

So does acceptance of our situation forbid change in our life? Is acceptance merely a polite word for depressed resignation at how things are for us? Is it just another way of saying 'Get used to it, buddy'?

Not at all. Acceptance is not opposed to change; instead acceptance brings a different energy to the situation.

Acceptance takes the heat of desire out of our future planning; it replaces wanting with a more primal energy comprised of transformed attitudes and new being; and in the face of these, even empires can crumble.

New being doesn't desire change; it is change.

The Ambassador's Shoes

The palace was in uproar, although more with laughter than rage. The newest ambassador had just presented himself to the Queen wearing filthy shoes, caked in the thickest chunks of mud!

A kind palace official took him to one side, and said, 'Your shoes, Sir?'

'What about my shoes?' said the ambassador. 'They are shiny and fine!'

'You perhaps haven't noticed that they're covered in mud?'

'Mud? Mud? I see no mud! I see only my reflection in the polished surface of the shiniest shoes in the land!'

We justify ourselves all the time. We imagine we are right in our imaginary battles. The present honesty of mindfulness will take us beneath these assumptions.

The official who raised questions about the ambassador's shoes was his friend – albeit a friend in disguise.

5

BECOMING
IMPERMANENT

*Ways to loosen, rather than
strengthen false securities.
We persist with some
unfortunate friendships.*

Our Thoughts Are Not Our Truth

Thoughts shoot from our minds like bullets from a gun – hard, shiny and lethal. And it is common for people to express their thoughts as though they are somehow true: 'It's self-evident to me that...'

Sometimes, I question people about this: 'You bestow great honour on your thoughts and imagine them very wise. But have you noticed how different they are when your mood changes? This week you attack me with your thoughts, yet last week you were kind to me with your thoughts and I haven't changed.'

We won't worship our thoughts, granting them grandiose authority in the moment. Instead, we'll watch them come and go like the muddle-headed busybodies they are, until eventually we tire of them.

Because muddle-headed busybodies are very tiring.

Reflections on a Small Fall of Snow

A thin quilt of snow was gently laid this morning.
Though, like the cream-fatness of the pre-dawn moon,
it will soon be gone and laid elsewhere.

For all is change,
and all is change,
and change is all, like snowy fall.

Apart from shift, adjustment and impermanent things,
for these don't change,
and these are always ours.

Sadly brief impermanence,
tragically dismantling impermanence,
green shoots of new life impermanence,

leading us home with unchanging care.

An Unfortunate Trio

Buddha saw greed, hatred and delusion as the root causes of humanity's problems.

Each emotion is destructive to relationships in different ways; and in ways you might recognize.

Greed moves *toward* relationships; it reveals itself in clinging anxiously to, or grasping at, established patterns. Greed is fear that change will lead to isolation or abandonment resulting in jealousy and, perhaps, an inability to tolerate small disconnections.

Hatred moves *against* relationships; it reveals itself in criticism and negative judgements resulting in anger, blame and, possibly, violence when frustrated. Hatred attempts to control others and maintain, at all costs, an imagined self-image.

Delusion moves *away* from relationships; it reveals itself in intellectualization, withdrawal, detachment and disassociation. Delusion results in inappropriate independence and denial in the face of vulnerability or yearnings for connection.

If any of these behaviours seems particularly familiar, it is helpful to loosen yourself from it.

Surfing the Waves

As we sit, we become aware of the different aspects of our present existence. We become aware, for instance, of our body, our feelings and our perceptions.

Perhaps we also discern the intentions and dispositions, which colour our mindscape; and sometimes, emerging from this mixed bag, there is consciousness.

We notice how, sometimes, all the aspects come together. Perhaps, for instance, we have toothache and we notice it causes distressed or irritated feelings. Our perception is that this pain is not temporary and, feeling distressed, an intention emerges to visit the dentist. Suddenly, aware of these processes unfolding in us, we become conscious.

What is apparent from this experience is how quickly these different aspects of our existence rise up and pass away. Like surfers riding the waves, we notice how we are picked up and put down by different energies all the time.

Why does this matter? Such awareness wonderfully undermines any attempts to make something solid or permanent out of my personal identity, out of 'me'.

Cloudy Vision

'I've learned to detach from my thoughts,' said a young woman. 'I observe them like clouds moving across the sky. Sometimes, I reach out and grab at them then I remember they're just passing and so I let them go. I feel much better for letting go of my thoughts because they drive me mad.'

Whenever we identify with an unpleasant thought or mood, we leave our true selves. These thoughts and moods are not who we are.

Treating our thoughts like the clouds in the sky, distant, passing, insubstantial...

well, this is like coming home.

The Sticking Point

Some students think the teacher is being unreasonable. He is holding up a stick in front of his class:

'Don't say to me "This is a stick",' he says, 'and don't say to me "This is not a stick". So tell me, what is it?'

The students are baffled and wonder what to say. They can't say it is a stick and they can't say it isn't. So just how do they reply?

Of course the teacher is demanding that they see beyond the labels we give to things and through to the essence of the object.

While on a walk recently, I was thinking about this incident. I had been throwing a stick for a Dalmatian, for whom it was a wonderful toy. On returning home, the stick became a mud-scraper, helping me remove the clinging clay from my boots. Once inside, my hosts lit a fire and the stick provided fuel for the fire, giving both light and warmth.

So what was this dear stick? And what am I?

The Garden

Next to the old monastery wall is a garden, loved into beauty by those who care for it. It's an idyllic spot in the early morning, with dew on the lawn and beds filled with flowers, their petals fresh with colour.

But as the monastery wall carries on round, the scene changes. Beyond the garden is a wasteland. Here the wall looks down on litter, empty cans of alcohol and drifters who find refuge here: a bleak port in the storm of their lives.

In time, things change. A few locals befriend the drifters and, together, they begin to bring life back to the wasteland. It's amazing how quickly friendship and hard work can change the character of the space.

In the idyllic garden, things are changing, too. When the gardener leaves for family reasons, things slip a little. The beds are not weeded as before and the lawn, in particular, suffers from a mysterious blight. It isn't the idyllic garden it once was.

Though I'm told there's a new gardener coming, who promises to bring fresh energy to the garden. The strange thing is that he used to be one of the drifters who lived on the wasteland next door.

How land, lives and seasons change.

'Is There Suffering in Paradise?'

We run hard from suffering, although we never quite leave it behind; for like the sun and the rain, all things need each other. To imagine we can have happiness without suffering is like wishing for a left hand without a right hand.

Suffering also brings the gift of compassion to the party. I notice that when I am sad, I am more likely to give charity to the homeless people that I pass on the street. My pain draws me to others that are in pain; I feel a tiny piece of what they feel.

Thich Nhat Hanh wrote: 'Paradise is not when there is no suffering; but where love and compassion exist. When suffering is there, it helps give birth to compassion.'

The Fruit

The fruit of mindfulness is awakening, a state in which greed, hatred and delusion are removed.

How does an awakened person live?

The awakened don't cease to be human. They still construct their moment-by-moment experience using their senses and perceptions; and they know both pleasure and pain.

But the difference is this: the experience of pleasure does not lead them to demand more pleasure; and the experience of pain does not create in them reactions of aversion and resistance.

The awakened have loosened their behaviour from the mode of self-interest. Untied from themselves, they become people with hands that are free to respond appropriately to events as they arise, expressing generosity (which is the opposite of greed), kindness (the opposite of hate) and understanding (the opposite of delusion).

Because the awakened don't exist, they exist ever more freely and ever more creatively. I describe your true self, of course.

A Friend Bearing Gifts

The world in which we live is a close friend that brings us gifts and, with each gift, there is fresh delight.

What is the present gift you hold in your hands? Perhaps, you are enjoying the first flush of romantic love or have been given a promotion at work or feeling proud for overcoming an obstacle.

And just as gifts arrive, they depart also. How could it not be so? No pleasure or possession is our birthright and we can't presume to own a particular pleasure, saying 'At last! I have it! Now it will always be so!'

Gifts are butterflies, which we receive joyfully and then joyfully release.

When we grip and cling on to gifts
they moulder and peel, like once-
bright paint in a damp house.

Knowing Better

Knowledge holds us back when we make it too permanent.

Meet a businessman called Michael, who does something rather strange. Whenever he attends board meetings, he brings Pickles along.

Who is Pickles?

Pickles is a large teddy that was once Michael's childhood friend. Michael sits him on the table, and takes him very seriously throughout the discussions.

A colleague asks Michael why he brings Pickles to everything. After all, he is now 42 years old, and a successful entrepreneur.

'How could I abandon him now?' says Michael, amazed that anyone should even ask the question.

'But you even consult with Pickles before making a decision!'

'He gets upset if I don't,' says Michael rather tetchily.

To learn something new every day, we must let go of something old every day. This is hard; for, like Michael, we are hoarders of old perceptions.

Beyond Thought

One of the reasons we remain stupid is our poor education.

We have been educated to think our way to truth, which is not helpful, because truth can't be thought.

This is why mindfulness doesn't engage with thought; there is nothing there for it to relate to.

Thought may begin by seeing but results in slavery – enslavement to concepts, which hack truth into thousands of ill-fitting pieces. We pluck a few of them from the air and imagine ourselves all-knowing.

Whole-mind can't be found in thought, because thought is split-mind. Truth exists in the spaces between thought, which is where the present takes us.

*Truth can't be communicated; it
just becomes apparent.*

God? Buddha? Penelope?

Some people pursue a name for themselves that will live on forever. Others cling onto names with special meaning: 'Ahh! That name is above all names!' they say.

But we'll be wary of getting caught up with names, whether they are 'God', 'Buddha', 'London' or 'Penelope', because as Lao-Tsu said, 'The name that can be named is not the true name.'

What, for instance, does the name 'Atlantic' tell us about the ocean? Nothing. So then we invent things, which we attach to the name; you invent your things and I invent mine and then we kill each other over it.

Names give only the impression of knowing. I can spell 'Atlantic' but I've never swum in it, so what do I know?

Exposing the Tough Guy

It is sometimes said that we don't possess an ego but are possessed by the idea of having one. I find this a helpful window onto truth, because it further diminishes the tough-guy reputation of our false personality, which turns out to be nothing more than an idea.

People often tell me that they are battling with their egos, as if it's all rather personal.

But it isn't personal. They're just noticing the death throes of an idea they once needed, but don't need any longer.

Now the role of your ego is similar to the role of leeches in medicine; not what it was.

Sadir Is Not Sadir

Sadir came to see me.

She had recently attended a retreat where she'd experienced glimpses of a freedom and joy previously unknown, though she hadn't experienced them since returning.

'I'm not being the person I could be!' she says in frustration. 'Can mindfulness help?'

'Mindfulness work begins with the uncritical observation of the person you imagine yourself to be,' I say.

'I don't need to imagine,' says Sadir. 'I know exactly who I am!'

'If you believe you're definitely Sadir,' I say, 'and that Sadir is definitely you, then you know nothing; you're asleep.'

Sadir is unhappy because she's fake. Sitting before me is an imagined self, an invented person; and what is not real can only attract fake thoughts and feelings.

The good news is that something in Sadir is trying to wake her. She has sensed that reality is not the same as her thoughts, and this is a life-changing discovery.

'I'm not the person I could be!' she says with frustration; and these are the first stirrings of a sleeping child.

The Cycle Path

On the path to awakening, the path out of sleep,
our day is a cycle.

It is a cycle of lost and found, lost and found;

a cycle of dying and rising, dying and rising;

a cycle of drowning and dry land, drowning and
dry land.

We will lose ourselves sometimes. We'll get caught
by a thought, which becomes a feeling that becomes
a mood. In this state, we are strangers to everything
except our obsession.

Here is our dying, which when noticed, becomes our
rising.

The awakened are those for whom dying and rising are
not so much words in a creed –

but daily experience of which they are aware.

The Breakwater

Like a seaside town flooded by a storm-tossed sea, so we can be overcome by circumstances.

It happens in different ways. Circumstances can creep up on us slowly and unnoticed; or hit us suddenly and savagely without warning.

We need to develop breakwaters against the surges of circumstance and, perhaps in time, a wall. Without these defences, we are constantly flooded, as life crashes through us and over us.

Each moment of mindfulness builds a little
more of the breakwater. As we return
to our breathing throughout the day,
the impact of these waves is diminished
and their impermanence exposed.

There's a Hole in My Bucket

We need a mind like a bucket of water with holes in it:

always emptying, not holding;

always returning to emptiness and to void.

Nirvana describes the ultimate loss of all notions: an absence of notions. This is not our normal state but it is our natural state.

With a mind like a leaking bucket, we gradually break attachments to the world we inhabit.

And find ourselves free to love it.

Thoughts on Happiness

Everyone wants to be happy but our notions of happiness don't always help us.

When, for instance, I write out a list of things that would make me happy, I immediately feel exposed, as I see before me a house of cards, which any gust of wind could destroy.

I say I need this or that to be happy and find myself becoming worried even as I write. I wonder if I shall ever obtain these desired things and contemplate the despair if I don't.

Yes, I am writing out my happiness list and becoming unhappy as I do it, which isn't the idea at all!

This makes me wonder if my notions of happiness are not helping me.

*What's on your happiness list? And
how does it make you feel?*

Mountainous John

John was an anxious man, who didn't believe he could cope with life in its present form. Events had taken a downward turn for him and, to cope with his anxiety, he had tried medication but it hadn't helped him.

He was a great lover of nature, however, and so when someone suggested that he contemplated a mountain, he was pleased to do so. Bringing the mountain into his consciousness for 15 minutes each day, his anxiety dissipated and was replaced by strength and a feeling of inner solidity.

'I've always loved mountains,' he said in his soft Irish accent. 'But I didn't realize I was a mountain!'

The world is one, and we are one with it,
and so we have more friends than we know
and more strength than we imagine.

Aloysia and the Door

It's not hard to feel her sense of abandonment.

Aloysia has just lost her boyfriend, who walked out on her without warning. She is also in a foreign country, because long ago she felt it necessary to take leave of her parents.

Her first reaction to this abandonment is to expend energy fighting off her true feelings, in order to defend her self. It is an exhausting fight and takes her nowhere.

After a few days, she becomes aware of this reaction; and she realizes it's been her default position ever since she was a small girl. She has never allowed herself to feel either angry or sad.

What will happen if she allows herself anger or sadness? She doesn't know. It's as if she's reached a door but it's shut; it has been closed all her life and she has no idea what lies beyond. She must now decide if she wishes to open the door.

Here, amidst the pain, is awareness of her present experience; awareness of her rejected feelings.

*If she can find trust and acceptance of
her state, the door will open by itself
and reveal all that is necessary.*

6

BECOMING
NOTHING

*Ways to allow space when
our tendency is to fill space.
Clutter is a health risk.*

When the Stadium Clears

As we focus on our breathing, it's like watching a stadium clear after a music gig or a football match.

As we breathe, in and out, we become aware of a crowd of emotions, thoughts and moods demanding attention; first one, then another. Here is resentment, there is envy, followed by a plan for later and then a memory of words spoken yesterday. What a crowd!

As we focus on our breathing, we realize what a mob of unchecked reactions are busy within us, and we can't simply stop them with a word of command.

We can remain unattached to them, however, merely by observing them as they pass through. And when we don't follow them; when we don't run after them and leap longingly into their arms; we find that they lose heart and give up.

Then it's like watching a stadium empty, until there is nothing, until we become no thing.

On the Plains of Nothing

We all have secret ideas of our value. We have daydreams and fantasies about how we'd like to be perceived; about who we are; about what is ours by right; and what will make us happy. These secret ideas pervade every moment of our day and every relationship.

In this way, our imaginary self drives and shapes our life. We attach happiness to images, which grip us like rings of steel. This is why we must leave the city of imagination, where such things thrive, and travel to the plains of nothing.

As you leave the city of imagination, the fantasy outfit you are wearing begins to fall from your body: first a shoe, then a coat, then a ring, and so on, until you are naked in the plains of nothing.

But, strangely, you are laughing for, although you feared being naked above all things, you have never felt better clothed.

The path to your true self does not run through the city of imagination.

Capacity for Life

It is a strange thing that as we empty ourselves, we become more solid people.

We sometimes say so-and-so is a 'big personality'. By this, we mean that his rage or her ambition or his need for attention or her opinions spill everywhere, filling the space within them and without.

These are not solid people, however, because there is no space there; and inner space determines our capacity for life.

If our space is filled by rage or ambition, by our need for attention or our opinions, there is no capacity in us for fresh creation or newness. We become like a newspaper that prints the same stories day after day – stale, with no capacity for anything but some distant yesterday.

As we breathe in space, and breathe out all else, we breathe in present strength and become solid people with capacity for living today.

If

Here's a suggestion:
instead of taking your self seriously,
take your absence of self seriously.

If you take your self seriously,
life will be both stressful and disappointing,
charged with greed, hatred and delusion –
for such things are the substance of self.

If, on the other hand, you take your absence of self
seriously,
then you will hold life more lightly,
touch life more joyfully,
and respond to it with more freedom and spontaneity.

If.

Greatness

It was an odd exchange, but maybe a telling one. The conversation took place between a man, who sat naked in his tub and had nothing, and Alexander the Great, who at that time ruled the world and had everything.

'I am greater than you are,' said the naked man in the tub.

'And why is that?' said Alexander.

'I have spurned more than you have seized. What you think is a great thing to possess is too trivial for me to scorn!'

The naked man's point was that those who can happily go without things, and don't require them, are happier than those who need to possess them.

As our needy self begins to lose its grip in our lives, so does the need to possess.

The passion to possess arises from my self's need for comfort and reassurance.

But what if my self doesn't exist?

The Space Man

When the space man arrived in the busy city, there were problems.

He was a strong man, and needed to be, as he dragged this wonderful space from town to town across the land. He liked to offer it to the busiest places, knowing if they lacked space that they would also lack tenderness.

But the space man was having trouble today because the Mayor said the space was too large to get into the city.

'It just won't fit,' said the mayor, scratching his head. 'The streets are too narrow and there are too many cars and people going about their business. I can hardly stop all this activity just for a bit of space. How about making it smaller?'

'You can't make space smaller,' said the space man, 'it's eternal.'

'But we've got things to do and lives to lead!' said the Mayor.

'Without space, there's no tenderness; and without tenderness, there's no life,' said the space man.

'Next year, perhaps,' said the mayor.
'This year's a write-off, but we'll try
and have some space next year.'

Where the Path Divides

Mindfulness is not concerned with your past.

In most therapeutic practice, the personal narrative of the individual is given considerable weight. The client is encouraged to tell their story and to reflect on the meaning they give to things. The therapist might then encourage them to look again at the narrative, and find new meaning in the material. Or perhaps explanations previously unnoticed will emerge, helping to explain current difficulties.

This is not the way of mindfulness, however. Indeed, mindfulness takes us away from such practice; away from discussions about our past or our future.

Instead, mindfulness seeks a transformation that is more primal and beyond words. It doesn't ask us to stir the pot of the past but, rather, to look through it and touch the place beyond, which is now.

Mindfulness is the quest not for a better self;
it is the quest for no self.

Good Company

It is wonderful to be with people who practise mindfulness truthfully.

One of the reasons they are such good company is the space they bring to the party. They possess an inner space, which can receive and hold all things offered, which makes them a gracious and healing presence.

This space is not present in all people. Sometimes, for instance, we raise an issue with a friend, but find ourselves pushed away. Instead of space, we experience a wall of resistance – suggesting the issue is touching something unresolved within them.

Our friend might react angrily, coldly or critically towards us; or perhaps we're just ignored. However we experience it, this lack of space in our friend is not a good experience.

Mindfulness practice works to enlarge our inner space; the 'no thing' out of which all things arise. We hold this space in our fluid lives and then take it with us, graciously, into the world.

Hold on to your inner space, it is more valuable than words can tell.

A Glimpse of Light

Elaine went on a weekend retreat to reflect on her life, which had not turned out as she'd hoped.

Her husband had left her, and their daughter would soon be going to college, leaving her alone. Without financial support, Elaine was facing having to sell her home of 20 years and downsize, and a smaller house meant losing many of her possessions.

And if she were to return to work after all this time, what would she do?

It was with these thoughts and fears that she left on retreat, but then enjoyed the most wonderful Sunday. Nothing in particular happened; it was just that from sunrise to sunset, she found peace in the light clear space of her surroundings. The ground was frosted and the sky was blue, which appeared to make it limitless in its capacity to hold.

These external circumstances became mirrored within her, as she experienced clear space, untroubled by concerns. It was remarkable how absent they were.

Though the day I saw her, it was cloudy; she was feeling trapped by the cloud and so were her worries.

The Forbidden Word

In the court of King Seed, in the country of Seedland, everyone knew the forbidden word. They knew it, because the King executed anyone who dared say it.

He was a brave king in many ways but, for some reason, this particular word made him tremble. So no one at court spoke it; and King Seed ruled his underground kingdom as best he could.

Until the day that one of the maids used the word in his hearing. She hadn't meant to; but someone had asked her the opposite of the word permanence and, without thinking, she'd shouted out, 'Impermanence, silly!'

'Who said that?' shouted King Seed. 'Who said impermanence?'

But before he could execute the girl – indeed, before he could say anything else at all – his small, shiny and hard body began to crack, fragment and transform, while everyone watched in amazement.

Some people think that talk of impermanence is depressing. No one thinks this in Seedland, where King Seed is now known as 'the Great Oak Tree of the Land Beyond'.

The Wisdom of Paint

Artists know this well.

They start with the intention, that which they wish to paint.

But embarking on the project, they soon experience resistance: the materials don't allow them to do what they wished, and their original intention proves unworkable.

Out of this crisis comes reconciliation. Here is a return to the spirit of the intention, but with the hindsight of experience something new emerges: a previously undreamed creation.

Like artists, we set out on life with intentions, only to lose many of them along the way. Due to resistance, in others or ourselves, these intentions don't or can't survive.

What then?

There are two options: we can choose shame, which like dripping acid takes up residence and quietly poisons all things. Or daily, we can create fresh space inside us: a nothingness in which our intentions and reality can be reconciled.

Out of fresh space an undreamed
masterpiece can emerge.

The Practice of Space

There is an important moment in the day, and let it be early. It is a sacred moment when I remember myself, gather myself; I feel my present breathing and the clean and clear space that is me.

Why does this practice matter? It helps me resist the subtle approaches of mechanical life, which daily threatens to ensnare me; the life of automatically reacting to events and people, which deprives me of compassion and spontaneity.

The sacred moment creates a sacred space. It's sacred because it is free from the madness of expectation and attachment and is therefore a space in which I am truly myself.

As the day proceeds, this space may be lost as I drift into the netherworld of automatic reaction. But sooner or later, with a whisper or a wallop, the space will wake me up.

As we practise returning to this space, we become less mechanical and more human –

which is delightful both for the world and me.

Spiritual Hell

No one is fond of people who love the external trappings of the spiritual life, without displaying the inner reality.

The Pharisees were famous for wanting to appear the most holy but they didn't impress Jesus and he called them 'white-washed tombs'.

The mystic Meister Eckhart was equally rude about such hypocrisy. Speaking of monks, whose egos found great pleasure in the excessive demands of penance and external devotion, he said, 'These people are called holy because of what they are seen to do, but inside they are asses! For they don't know the real meaning of the divine truth.'

And in our generation, the burgeoning popularity of the self-help movement has created fresh possibilities for the ego. In holier-than-thou zeal, people distract themselves with life-changing books and life-changing conferences, only to remain the same.

The ego thrives, whenever we strive. If we desperately desire this, or passionately desire that, then our ego will be in seventh heaven.

Will nothing. Desire nothing.
Leave nothing for your ego to work on.

The Danger of Old Maths

Sometimes our maths can make us unhappy.

Our emotional state is the sum of two things: an external event and an internal feeling about our past. Surprised?

You'll notice I don't say 'an internal feeling about the event', but an internal feeling about our *past*. You know this from the way people behave. It's not the event itself that matters.

For one person, conflict is a terrible experience; for another, it is barely noticed.

Some, however rich, will spend their whole life fearing being poor while others, however poor, will never worry about money.

For one person, the opinion of others is crucial; for another, it is less so.

What do we learn from these things? We learn that current events are not experienced purely, but with attitudes from the past. If we're wise, therefore, we don't take our reactions too seriously, but begin to loosen ourselves from the effects of old feelings.

This is the only maths that adds up.

Quietening the Scream

The loudest scream in the West is the scream for self-esteem.

Amidst the rampant individualism of Western society, huge pressure is placed on each person to be something. We are not people whose identity is safely held as part of a community. Rather, we are those who must do it for ourselves; be it for ourselves.

The emergence of our celebrity culture is just a small part of this illness; narcissism is written deep into every layer of our social environment. We are happy when something or someone makes us feel good about ourselves; we are unhappy when this is not the case.

Mindfulness practice is concerned with freeing us from this treadmill. Rather than affirming your self, which will always find new ways to be unhappy, it seeks rather to illuminate the self's lack of substance; its ghost-like qualities.

Once we're in the hills, beyond the battle for self-esteem, our screaming quietens.

On the Other Side of Depression

There is a heaviness about depression that needs lightening;

a fog that needs clearing;

a surliness that needs dissolving;

a despair that needs lifting;

an anger that needs melting;

a slothfulness that needs enlivening;

and a delight that needs finding.

The opposite of depression is not happiness;

it is vitality.

The Real Magic

We applaud when the magician makes a rabbit disappear; but let us save the heartiest applause for when we disappear.

Why? Let's go backstage and consider how you were made.

The birth of your self, as you know it, was not a happy one. Your self was not made from love or care but from your mind grabbing at perceptions from 'the untrammelled flow of phenomena' around you. This collection of perceptions about our self, we call 'me'.

And here begins a vicious circle: your random perceptions become your self; and your self, the guardian of these perceptions, generates thoughts. These thoughts congeal into beliefs, which then influence your perceptions.

Agghh!

It's not a pretty picture and 'Let me out of here!' is a natural response to this claustrophobic creation.

So applaud the magician when the rabbit disappears; but save your heartiest applause for when you disappear.

Just like that! Or however long it takes...

The Goal Is No Goal

The happy person seeks no particular outcome from what they do; only the unhappy do this. And they're unhappy because they insist on outcomes that rarely occur.

An act undertaken with a particular end or goal in mind is an act of misery; it is a mercenary in the world, paid by desire and self-love and with no heart of its own.

Alternatively, we can intend nothing by our acts. We can shun agendas and pay no heed to applause or reward.

Peel away the clinging ivy of desire and let your actions go free in the world, and you will find that they are not mercenaries at all but have the freshness of morning dew and lead to endless possibilities.

When no thing is the goal, it is possible
our acts become some thing, because
they emerge pure in the world.

The Nameless Ones

The stationmaster was called Ralph, and proved very helpful, telling me the train information I needed. I spotted him easily; his uniform revealed his identity as an employee of the train company.

Of course, that's not Ralph's only identity. Like all of us, he has many identities. Perhaps he is a father and a stamp collector and a keen follower of ice dancing. He is probably a son and maybe a brother. He could be a school governor or a supporter of a football club. Perhaps he is Welsh, plays in a band and is a friend to someone. Perhaps he is a man who gives money to people on the street.

So many identities beyond his station uniform! That just happens to be how I meet him and how he is helpful to me today.

And beyond these identities, Ralph has no identity because space can't be named. You can't pin a label on space, for there is nothing to hold the pin. We become things for people, as Ralph did for me; but we don't become what they want us to be.

This is why each day, whatever uniform we wear or role we play, we start as the nameless one.

Pure space.

Acceptance

A person who has strong dislikes, and justifies them – this person does not realize their own nothingness.

They are taking their personality too seriously given that its advice is always unhelpful.

It is good to work on dislikes but first we allow them to become apparent; first, we observe them

with acceptance.

Light in a Dark Future

Knowing things is highly valued in society. But we're never better placed than when we're unknowing, and so we can allow ourselves to be there.

Unknowing is not a popular destination. Sometimes people say, 'I am quite in the dark about my future!' Or, 'I don't know what will happen!' These are not happy statements and arise from fear of unknowing.

Unknowing needn't be feared, however, for here is a state of receptivity; a place of emptiness, which has the potential for filling. A hand holding one thing can't receive another and, equally, a place already full can't be filled again.

So although knowing is highly valued in society, we're never better placed than when we're unknowing.

Relax now and allow yourself there.

Allergic Reactions

I am allergic to large words like 'Buddha', 'God' and 'Love'.

They bring me out in a rash; make me feel nauseous.

They are the pegs on which we hang our hypocrisy, possessiveness, insecure arrogance and pomposity.

If you mention these words, I may have to leave the room in disgust and to save myself from going mad.

Instead, let's talk about real things,
like your walk to work or your choice
of picture in the front room.

Why Those Who Search Find Nothing

We must be careful that our searching does not stop us finding. Searching means having a goal, which can make us blind to everything else.

There was once a man called Carlton who wanted to be rich; this was his passion and his goal. One day, he goes out for a walk longing to discover ways to be wealthy.

By the side of the road is a beggar, who is giving away large gold coins, but Carlton walks straight past him. If Carlton took the coins he'd be instantly rich but he doesn't see the beggar, even though he walks within inches of his nose.

Why doesn't he see him? The answer is simple: if your goal is to be rich, you don't pay attention to beggars. Why would you? What have they got to do with your search?

This is why we are careful that our searching does not stop us finding.

Carlton would have benefited from searching less and noticing more.

7

BECOMING
ONE

*Ways towards union when
our tendency is separation.
It is about dismantling walls.*

Oneness in a Dual World

At the heart of Buddhist teaching is non-duality or the oneness of existence.

The English poet John Donne put it another way: 'No man is an island entire of itself,' he wrote, 'every man is a piece of the continent; a part of the main.'

In a dual world, things are separated by labels and set against each other: good against bad, you against me, my ideas against your ideas, man against woman, this country against that country and so on. You are familiar with the outcomes.

In a non-dual world, in a world that is one, things can't be set against each other. I can't be against you because I am you.

In Donne's day, the tolling of the village bell indicated a death and people were sent to find out the name of the deceased, to find out for whom the bell tolled. But as he continued in his famous meditation, there is a bigger truth here:

> *'Each man's death diminishes me,*
> *For I am involved with mankind.*
> *Therefore, send not to know*
> *For whom the bell tolls,*
> *It tolls for thee.'*

The Eternal Exchange

Have you ever felt yourself getting smaller?

When we meet a person who has smallness of understanding, we too can become small. However much we try not to be, we are drawn into their smallness.

When we meet a person, however, in whom there is largeness of understanding then we too become large. We are received by their largeness, which then becomes ours.

So we'll be aware of those people that fill our days; for in spiritual terms, one thing is always in another. You are in your boss, your dog, your child, your newsagent – and they are in you.

Smallness in another brings out the smallness in me, while largeness in another brings out the largeness in me.

That which receives is the same as that which is given, for it receives nothing other than itself –

in an eternal exchange of being.

My Walk to the Shops

I set out on a walk to the shops, hoping the world will be kind.

For the first fifty yards I am not helped by my attitude, which sees everything and everyone as separate from me. The people are separate, the trees are separate and the clouds are separate.

Once noticed, this sense of separation dissolves. All aspects of my environment are me and I am them. I feel a strong sense of blessing in this shared existence and an inner alteration that brings a smile to my face. Something seemed very important when I left home, but I can't remember what it was now.

I talk to a woman on the corner. After some pleasant conversation, I notice an irritated reaction arising in me. I allow it to pass through before it becomes self-justification, which is never good news.

In all this, I am helped by the endless shift and change of the clouds, as they form and reform, high in the sky.

Pond Life

I am reminded of myself today, while looking in a large fishpond.

Here are many fish, all shapes and sizes, darting this way and that in a colourful, lively and unpredictable display.

From a distance, the pond looked calm and settled; but close up, I see only movement and change. Here is constant process with nothing fixed but the pond walls; and here I see myself.

We are more state than trait, as they say. We change constantly in relation to our circumstances, as our circumstances change in relation to us. However many times a person comes to see me, I have never met the same person twice.

And such fluidity of being bodes well for happiness. Our dissolving sense of a self diminishes our capacity for offence; for there's much less of us to be offended.

When our self dissolves, our painful struggle for self-aggrandizement also loses force; for which self are we aggrandizing?

The fishpond only looks static from a distance; and we only look static to a fool.

A Big Step

It's like stepping from the Earth to the moon.

It's a big step.

I'm talking of the moment in our lives when we can accept the difficult bits of ourselves.

We can embrace the happy bits easily enough; but can we be kind to our more discomforting and negative reality?

It's good if we can... because everything has its place.

I'm reminded of rotting fruit in the compost which becomes a significant catalyst for new growth.

The soil of your existence needs it all, the difficult and the easy; the awkward and the presentable.

Everything belongs.

Can you live that today?

Yes, everything belongs.

The Intruder

My early morning runs are painful at present, so I go to see my osteopath.

My osteopath tells me that I have torn some muscles in my leg; but I am wondering if I have a hernia, too. We can't be sure yet, but I fear this may be true. I don't want a hernia, because I enjoy running and might have to wait a long time for the operation.

As I breathe, I am conscious only of my body, listening for the signs. This is how it is when you don't want something; the dread can dominate.

Soon, however, I stop wishing the hernia away and accept my present experience. 'Welcome, brother hernia!' as St Francis might say. 'And what message do you bring for me today?'

If I have a hernia, then this intruder must become a guest in my body; no more pushing away what is part of me.

I breathe in acceptance; I breathe out rejection.

Approaching Truth

It's best if we don't approach truth in an adult way.

Adults like to sort things out. They have debates, in which both sides of the argument are considered, and one side declared the winner. This is how the adult thinks and adults place great store by their thoughts.

Consequently, in the truth market, this is how truth is wrapped and sold. Truth is spliced, packaged and displayed for thought-buyers; and sold as certainties to the insecure.

But not everyone leaves the market satisfied. The adult is happy enough, feeling justified in their choices, but the child remains restless, unhappy and unfed.

The child, you see, hasn't learned how to splice truth, knowing it only as one; and can't rest until all is complete again.

It is a good day when we stop buying off-cuts from the truth market; until then, the child cries.

Squeezing the Satsuma

I live above a greengrocer and his shopfront is wonderfully full of fresh fruit and vegetables.

The morning delivery arrives around 5 a.m. and the fruit stacked high is a fine sight, though I remain a discerning buyer.

I squeeze the satsumas, check the apples, feel the tomatoes and ponder the mushrooms. He is a good greengrocer, but the quality of the produce can vary so it's wise to be vigilant.

And today, as I practise awareness of present experience with acceptance, I will also be vigilant for the varying quality of my thoughts and feelings. Any of them which serve to separate me from another, I will greet with a smile – but leave on the shelf.

They are yesterday's delivery.

Leaving the Prison

'A human being,' said Einstein, 'is part of the whole, which we call the Universe; a part limited in time and space. He experiences himself, his thoughts and feelings, as something separate from the rest – a kind of optical delusion of consciousness. This delusion is a kind of prison for us, restricting us to our personal desires and to affection for a few persons nearest to us. Our task must be to free ourselves from this prison by widening our circle of compassion to embrace all living creatures and the whole of nature in its beauty.'

For those wishing to leave the prison of delusion, the only task is the wall-melting and life-expanding practice of present awareness with acceptance.

It is a state in which deluded and separate boundaries cannot exist.

A Turner Sky

The other day, as I walked mindfully in the city, I looked up and saw a 'Turner' sky: the sort of luminous sky that the English Romantic landscape painter J.M.W. Turner looked at so profoundly and painted so well.

And, for that moment, time melted away, personality blurred and we were one and the same person, William and I, looking up at one and the same sky.

The eternal now does not know our distinctions.

And Sometimes Passers-by

Good words, when I am able to become one with them, strengthen me, calm me and hold me. Better than a warm coat, they are like a fire within, as I become one with them and their meaning. It is a moment of unity, which makes me bigger than any anxiety, fear or rage that is loitering inside. The wooden arrows they shoot bounce off me.

We will be aware of that with which we become one today, whether a word, mood, person or idea; we'll be aware of how they shape us. We'll seek unity with that which makes us larger people and be passers-by of those things that make us small.

Yes, sometimes we will be passers-by.

The Manuscript

Lorna, the historian, is struggling with the manuscript and is in some despair.

How she longs to read it! This manuscript has been lost for centuries, but now it's found, there's disappointment. For here in the casket is not one piece of paper, but a thousand or so pieces. Someone has torn up this priceless piece of writing! And whereas once it was simple to read, it is now very hard.

The manuscript was not written to be a problem; the words were written clearly on a single parchment. And so quietly, Lorna sits down to return it to its original state.

Multiplicity of thought and emotion is like a thousand knives within us. The blades shred truth and make it hard for us to read. Isolated fragments, away from the whole, become nonsense; and on this nonsense, we build.

*In our breathing today, we remember
Lorna and her manuscript. Where there is
multiplicity, let simplicity settle; let the simple
whole, where the truth of our lives is clearly
written, be there in our deepest breath.*

Where Is Home?

There is a strong sense of coming home in mindfulness.

As we look at things presently, everything and everywhere is home – the seat on the bus, the air we breathe, the people we meet, the desert cave... And as we look at things presently, we find also that we are made up of other things.

Thich Nhat Hanh, a contemporary poet and Zen master, reflects memorably on oneness as being like a wave, saying that if a wave looks deeply into her self, she discovers she is made of other waves. She is not a separate event surging forward, but a partnership with every other wave in the sea.

When we look presently, when we look deeply, everywhere is relationship and everywhere is home.

No End to Our Beginning

The word 'Nirvana' describes the reality of no birth and no death, and is our substance, just as air is the substance of the wind.

The word 'God' describes the ground of our being, and is our substance, just as flame is the substance of fire.

Just as we can't ascribe a beginning or end to Nirvana or God, so we can't ascribe such things to ourselves, for they are our substance –

like water is the substance of the sea.

Substantial and Insubstantial

There are two figures inside us: substantial and insubstantial.

You will recognize substantial, because in its care you are strong and calm: present, aware and accepting. Insubstantial is different, comprised of different voices seeking your attention, which come and go with alarming speed.

What sort of voices do you hear? If you are experiencing resentment, bitterness, fear, jealousy, panic, depression, anxiety, irritation, hostility or confusion then insubstantial is handling your affairs.

Substantial looks after insubstantial; great kindness and patience are shown, for they are close. And as time goes by, the wounding power of negative feeling fades, the two become ever more one.

Until, one day, there is just substantial you.

The Hostage

A hostage counsellor said some interesting words when a victim was released recently.

The hostage had endured several mock executions but seemed relatively strong as he reflected on his experiences. The counsellor listened to the interview with the hostage and was asked what he made of the hostage's emotional state.

'How people leave the hostage experience is how they went into it,' he replied.

His meaning was clear. If they took strong inner resources with them into the nightmare, they would leave with those resources strengthened. If they took few resources with them, they may leave with even what they had shattered.

Strength is an exchange. If we offer strength to a situation, it is offered back.

Sometimes I stand by a resilient tree in the winter wind. The tree is me and I am the tree; we offer each other strength.

Walking Mindfully

Mindful walking is not the same as thoughtful walking, though, from a distance, they might look the same.

A thoughtful walk exists somewhere other than the present. Perhaps we're reflecting back on a person or event or imagining forward to a possible outcome.

Mindful walking is not like this, because it is the present experience of our selves through direct experience of the environment.

As I walk, here is the paving stone and here is the tree and here is the warehouse and here is the old door and here is the lamp post; and they are speaking to me directly for they are as I am and I am as they are.

Perhaps I am addressed by the spaciousness of the warehouse or the tree buckling; maybe the resilience of the paving stone speaks to me, or the door being locked or the lamp post offering light.

But I am not addressed in words, for awareness is prior to language. Instead, their being becomes my being, and my being their being in direct converse.

This is who I am now. I have no other existence.

A Touching Story

Sometimes small boys have to entertain themselves.

While his mum is talking to the man on the stall, the small son is inventing a game. Facing out toward the pavement, he is touching everyone who passes by.

Now most people are too busy or too big too notice, though an older boy does and glances back at him with a look of youthful disapproval that says *What do you think you're doing?*

Sally has watched the little boy for a while and now she approaches him. His mother is still talking to the man on the stall and he is still reaching out to passers-by, touching each as they hurry on.

When Sally reaches him, she catches his eye, stretches out her hands and says, 'High fives!' The boy understands immediately and brings his hands up to meet hers with excitement in his eyes.

Though there is probably more excitement
in Sally, because union is like that.

Riverside Tales

When you contemplate a river, you contemplate a life that is everywhere all at once.

Here in the moment, it is a trickling source in the hills, a slow-moving middle course and a flowing out to sea at the mouth. It is rapids, waterfall and calm procession; and it is all these things at once.

The river is everywhere and every way and present; its beginning, middle and end are all now.

And as with the river, so with us, the seven ages of the human in the moment; from birth to death, not separated by time but everywhere and all things at once and now.

There's no time but the present.

The Picture Cutter

The man was eventually imprisoned, so we've got to the end of the story in the opening line.

What did he do? I'll tell you. He used to cut up pictures.

'Why do you do that?' asked his cleaner one day.

'I just take the bits I want,' he replied. 'Who needs the rest?'

He cut up all kinds of pictures, which he found in newspapers and magazines, both masterpieces and new works. He'd take a bit from one and a bit from another and then put them in his 'feel-good' drawer.

However, he never had time to enjoy his 'feel-good' drawer, because he was busy cutting out further bits he wanted.

'Don't you ever want the whole picture?' asked the cleaner.

'The whole picture has too much that I don't want,' he said.

The man was imprisoned not by the courts, of course, but by his inability to relate to anything, which didn't make him feel good.

He didn't want the whole picture;
he just wanted his picture.

When the Truth Gets Heated

Firewatchers know many joys.

A particular pleasure of watching a fire is the unfolding union of difference, as a spark becomes a flame becomes the wood becomes the fire in a stunning exchange of energy and form.

I regard myself as fortunate when I'm able to witness this and almost uncomfortably close to heaven.

I don't have answers when it comes to fires. Who can say where the spark ends and the flame begins? And who can say where the wood ends and the fire begins? They are not the same but they are one; the flame holds the spark just as the wood is the fire.

I take the heat of this union into a world cold
with mental boundaries and walls that declare:
'I'm not you and you're not me!'

Contented?

The woman is telling me how contented she is.

'I'm very contented,' she says. 'Very, very contented.'

I ask if she ever gets angry. She says people dying in Afghanistan make her angry.

Why that war in particular?

'Because we shouldn't be there!' she says testily

She is smiling quickly again however, and adds: 'But I'm able to push that stuff away and stay contented!'

And as she says this, she pushes away an imaginary irritant with her hands, enacting with her body what she is doing in her mind.

I feel uncomfortable. I suggest that it isn't true contentment if she needs to reject unwanted emotions in order to maintain it.

'Why not inhale your anger and exhale your fear of anger?' I say. 'Perhaps then you could talk of contentment more truthfully.'

She moves away.

Touching Presence

Sometimes we touch it in ourselves.

We touch pure presence, and know that we are well and whole and one.

Like a baby at peace, no crying here but sweet calm; and there is nothing to be said, and nothing which can harm, and nothing desired, and everything understood in the eternal moment.

Sometimes.

8

BECOMING
BEHAVIOUR

*Ways to respond to the world, when
our tendency is to react to the world.*

Body of Evidence

Beware of your body hypnotizing you.

Sometimes our bodies hypnotize us into a particular state. It might be our facial muscles being unhelpful, as they scowl or harden; or our taut wrist muscles, jutting jaw, twitching legs, stooped shoulders, pushed-out chest, tense shoulders or darting eye movements.

Our body can hypnotize our emotional mood. If, for instance, we stop frowning, our mechanical anger might disappear; or if we stop our quick anxious movements, our anxiety might begin to fade.

Sometimes our moving centre - which controls our bodies - can hypnotize our emotional centre or thinking centre, and perpetuate a negative emotion by continuing to act it out, long after it should have passed through us.

It appears that some people's bodies have sealed-in emotions for life. Don't give such power to your body today. Notice the games it plays, the old ways it lives out and ask it to relax when necessary.

Your body is your companion,
not your hypnotist.

I'm Not Always Mindful

Mindfulness is present awareness of our unedited selves with acceptance.

We're mindful when we're aware of what's passing through us – pleasant or otherwise – and allow it to be so, just as it is... like we allow the passing clouds.

We may lose this mindful state.

A thought or emotion will kidnap us, maybe for minutes, hours or days; or we'll put ourselves in the way of distraction, hopping from this to that, like a restless butterfly.

And that's all right.

Mindfulness is not suddenly and permanently acquired... but something we grow into.

It's the slow recovery of our endlessly present soul.

Perhaps we're more mindful of our lives than once we were?

We're on the way.

'I'm Listening'

Only a few have the capacity to listen.

Only a few know how to allow another's words to enter their mind; how to remain quiet, open and waiting whatever the nature of the flow, whether a torrent or a trickle.

In listening such as this, each word is greeted and weighed, and no word lost through distraction or · turned away in impatience.

No word is praised and no word is rebuked; no word applauded and no word judged.

Such a listener will have their own story, their own search – but that is not present in the space offered by the one who is aware, present and accepting.

When you discover such a listener,
you discover treasure.

Letting Go

Hot cups are similar to perceptions.

If a cup of hot tea is burning your hands, then let go of it. The cup may smash on the floor and spill tea everywhere: better the mess of a broken cup than burned hands.

Were you to cling stubbornly to the scalding cup, whether in ignorance or fear, it would be foolish. Letting go of something that causes you suffering is prudent.

In the same way, let go of perceptions that cause you suffering, for they hurt you more than a scalding cup. Perceptions are hurtful because they are often mistaken or misinformed and, through them, you become vain, self-righteous or negative.

How might you start? You already have, once mindfulness reveals the impermanent and discredited nature of your current obsession.

So you let go.
You let go.
You let go.
And then you let go again.

Anxiety Issues

Some people call anxiety a problem but this isn't quite true.

Fighting anxiety is the problem... because symptoms only intensify when we try to get rid of them.

The more I insist I fall asleep, the more I don't.

The genius here is to grow into acceptance of my body and mind, and the variety of experiences they offer.

So things continue to arise, echoes of my past... but they don't overwhelm.

And progress is measured not by an absence of panic... but by how much anxiety I can allow.

We can say something like:

'I'm not anxious; it's not who I am.
I'm merely experiencing anxiety.
Some unresolved material from my past is
passing through, visiting... but not staying.'

Marcos and the Parachute

A young skydiver called Marcos is hurtling towards the ground. Suddenly his instructor is alongside him, telling him to remove his unused parachute.

His first thought is: *What's going on?*

His second thought is: *This is completely ridiculous!*

His third thought makes him feel angry with the instructor: *Everything is going well. Why is he messing up my skydive?*

The instructor persists with his request and Marcos persists with his refusal until, suddenly, Marcos' precious parachute pack is wrenched from him and jettisoned by the instructor.

Marcos now has nothing as he falls downwards. Panic shoots through his body, until the instructor hands him another parachute, one he hadn't seen.

They both land safely, after which Marcos discovers that his original parachute was one of a faulty batch and couldn't be trusted.

We won't fear the loss of our illusions.
We cling to illusion but letting go
doesn't lead to disillusionment – simply
a safer landing and a better way.

Closing the Door

'I, too, closed the door,' he said, and I was shocked.

Here is the nub of the matter in this short piece: we forgive people because we are the same as them.

When angered by someone, it's helpful to consider the attitude in the other that causes your rage; and then to see whether this attitude is ever in you. What am I angry at? When I reflect in this way, I never fail to find the offending attitude also in me.

I remember someone reflecting on the Holocaust and talking about the guards who closed the doors of the gas chambers on millions of innocent lives.

'I, too, closed the doors,' he said, and I was shocked.

Born years after the end of World War II, I knew he had never been near the gas chambers. He understood, however, that in different ways, he'd treated people as nothing, whether in thought or deed. He had snuffed out innocence, too.

We don't forgive because we are better
but because we are the same.

The Origins of Yoga

The evening yoga class takes many forms these days.

In its original sense, yoga was concerned with yoking body and mind, like two wild horses brought together, and binding them to the will. Our will is the seat of change; what we will, we do.

So yoga includes ascetic practice, which denies the body or mind something it craves. By doing this, we feel the impatient textures of desire in our body but also feel through them to freedom beyond.

Yoga also uses meditation, which reduces personal ignorance and grows self-knowledge, by allowing us to witness the unfolding patterns of body and mind, as they occur. In particular, we face our toxic thoughts, darting through us like frightened fish.

So yoga, as originally conceived, trains our will to save us from the power of grabbing desire and the deep fog of personal ignorance.

Quite enlightened, really.

Stoned

I see the strangest thing today. At the shopping mall, I watch a crowd of people place stone after stone on a man's body, crushing the life out of him. The man is still alive and struggling, though no one seems concerned.

I run across towards them.

'What are you doing?' I ask.

'Nothing,' they reply, 'just a normal day.'

'Just a normal day! But what about the stones?'

'What stones?' they exclaim with genuine surprise before continuing with their work.

Equally, we are blind as we load other people with our agendas, with what we want from them. And each desired outcome is a heavy stone on their soul.

If we are to practise one thing today it could be stone-removal, as we allow people to get up and go free.

Set free and you shall be set free.

Doing the Impossible

Today, we will do the impossible. We will be both someone who cares and someone who doesn't care.

'Teach us to care and not to care,' wrote T.S. Eliot, and this is a helpful saying, because doing one without the other is dangerous.

So today we allow compassion to the surface and, perhaps, we will help someone in some way.

We'll remain mindful, however, that our help doesn't become a claim over another; or perhaps, a mark of our skill or kindness.

We don't offer care to bolster our self-image or self-esteem; this is narcissism dressed up as virtue.

This is why we let go of our care before it has even left us, barely aware of it passing through.

'Teach us to care and not to care.'

Ever-diminishing Reflections

Each day, we break off a little piece of the mirror.

Our mirror may start large and take pride of place.

Daily we stand in front of it, placing great significance on its reflected assessment.

Sometimes we grant significance to the assessments of others, which can be another mirror that oppresses.

Neither of these are helpful mirrors.

So each day, we break off a little piece of the mirror. We do this until there is so little left that we give up looking at ourselves – whether through our eyes or those of others – and simply enjoy being ourselves.

Enjoy life away from the mirrors.

An Empty Bowl

Our love is to be an ambitious love, seeking not the happiness of a select few but the happiness of many.

Such daring love needs nurture, however, and we'll require a strong base or refuge on this adventure, whether it's a community, a teaching or a simple practice of our own. It could be all three.

If alone, we might invent a ritual.

Sometimes I hold an empty bowl at the start of the day. I breathe in simplicity and space, and breathe out multiplicity and confusion.

At other times I use a crystal glass I was given. I wish for myself and the world, the end of delusion and the coming of joy, and then I ring the glass and allow the healing sound to fill my room and then the world.

As you hear the call to ambitious love,
you will find your own refuge, ritual
and strength for the adventure.

By the Waters of Babylon

Have you met people like this?

They live abroad but keep glancing back at the place they left. They didn't mean to leave but somehow they have gone. They thought it was to be for a short while, but short has now become long.

And, though they constantly declare how happy they are, there is a sigh in their breath and a sense of exile within; they feel cut off from their homeland.

'By the waters of Babylon we sat down and wept when we remembered Zion,' wrote the psalmist, describing the pain of the Jews in exile in Babylon. There were no pretend smiles here.

When we leave our inner ground, we join those in exile. Our inner ground is our home ground. The truth is always in our own ground and not beyond it, in some other person or place.

So today we'll notice each call to get into someone else's line, each demand that we dance to another's tune, each invitation into exile. And who knows? Maybe we'll go there, before returning in time to our own ground.

Until one day we stay, never to leave again, home for good.

Secrets of Fire-eating

I was watching a fire-eater recently.

The origins of fire-eating lie in India but, wherever it is practised, there's no such thing as 'cold fire'. The secret of fire-eating is simply enduring the pain – and the ability to tolerate constant blisters on your tongue, lips and throat.

The most famous fire-eater in history was probably Robert Powell, who lived in the seventeenth century. He would swallow fire, red-hot coals and melted sealing wax, and he appeared in front of British and European royalty for nearly sixty years.

But royalty or not, and despite all his experience, there was no 'cold fire' for Robert, no slick trick of avoidance.

We breathe into the pain, not around it.

Meister Eckhart in His Own Words

SP: What is the most powerful form of prayer?

ME: The most powerful form of prayer, and one which can gain almost all things and which is the worthiest work of all, is that which flows from a free mind.

SP: That's very quotable. And a free mind can achieve all things because it is not tied to any particular outcome?

ME: A free mind is one that is quite untroubled and unfettered by anything; a mind that has not tied itself to any way of being or devotion, and does not seek its own interest in anything.

SP: Now there's a challenge.

ME: Rather, it is forever immersed in God's most precious will, having left its own. There is no work, which men and women can perform, however small, that does not draw its strength from this leaving of its power and strength.

What wind fills your sails today?

Our Community

It is important to maintain our community.

We all live in a community. Whoever we meet or have dealings with, they are our community. If you meet a street cleaner every morning on your run, he is part of your community.

People come and go in our lives, whether they are family, work colleagues or our newsagent.

But we always nurture the present community with kindness. We help them when, unknowingly, they don't help us; as they help us when, unknowingly, we don't help them.

Whatever its shape or form – and no two are the same – there is safety in your community and blessing.

You are their home and they are yours.

Mindful Listening

When someone listens to us, it's one of the best experiences in the world. Sadly, some people have never been listened to, leaving much hurt sealed inside.

They may have had countless conversations – banter, gossip, shouting matches, hilarity and keen debate – but they've never been listened to; and their life never heard. This, of course, is why polite conversation makes people feel depressed. Polite conversation isn't listening.

Mindfulness improves the quality of our listening by freeing energy. Energy, formerly wasted on controlling situations or defending our own position, now becomes available for listening.

Mindfulness also bestows tranquillity. In ourselves, we learn to allow whatever arises; and so we learn to allow this in others, too. People know we'll be undisturbed by whatever is revealed, which helps them feel safe with us.

And mindfulness bestows concentration; that sustained quality of focus, nurtured in our daily practice of returning ourselves to the present. There is no distraction in the present, and so we're able to offer our full attention.

When it comes to listening, some offer only minimal presence. Described here, though, is optimal presence: truly one of the great wonders of the world.

Mindful Leadership

'Office relationships have changed recently,' says my friend. 'It's all become much more unpleasant.'

Why? Her boss is too full of their own stuff to hold anyone else. And good leadership is holding.

When we don't feel held, like babies, we panic and turn on those around us.

So in the office, everyone is now looking out for themselves; and there's bitching as well.

'Even I've started being bitchy and I don't want to be,' she says.

Mindful leadership first pays attention to itself:

'What is arising in me today? What thoughts or feelings dominate?'

If I can notice these, I become better able to pay attention to others.

Self-awareness loosens the grip of our own internal patterns and creates space that can be offered to others.

The mindful boss will always be able to say, 'My door – and my mind – is open. If it matters to you, it matters to me.'

The Unhappy Daffodil

The daffodil was making itself unhappy.

Because it had a green stem, the daffodil looked at a green bus full of people and thought: *I could be as green and popular as that bus.*

And because the daffodil could grow in springtime, it looked at the much-admired crocus and thought: *Well, I can grow in spring as well, you know!*

And because it was good at being yellow, the daffodil gazed at the sun, which people so loved, and thought: *Being yellow is easy. I don't know why the sun gets all the credit!*

The daffodil was forgetting that it was best at being a daffodil – the bus, crocus and sun could only dream of being so glorious.

A Seafront Table in Winter

I am in a seaside town in winter, walking along the seafront before the world wakes. The seaside cafés are closed and quiet in the cold but I notice a frosty table, which someone forgot to put away.

In the summer, this table would be busy and useful. People would hover to get a seat, waiting for someone to move. The table would be in demand, holding tea and cakes, milkshakes and ice cream or, perhaps, servings of fish and chips.

In the winter dawn, things are different. The table is alone, sought by no one and touched by frost. It's beautiful but not useful - though I note a sea gull alighting upon it for temporary rest before returning to the chill currents of the sky.

I sometimes feel the need to be useful, because it makes me feel better about myself. When it isn't the season, it is hard and it's during these times that I try to force things and insist on being useful; when all the time, like the seafront table, it's enough to be touched by beauty.

Perhaps, just being beautiful is useful.

Let's Not Call It Love

Let us now talk of love beyond the nonsense fields.

Love is made of understanding; this is its substance. Love understands another's hopes and fears, frailties and longings and, out of such understanding, comes tenderness and compassion.

Love is a spacious affair. Love allows for coming and going, for it knows nothing of possessiveness.

And, arising from the deep places, there will always be the bubbling spring of delight, for as Thich Nhat Hanh observed: 'If both parties cry every day, that is not true love.'

We talk of love beyond the nonsense fields.

The Daily Death

Death, our daily calling, is the removal of possession from our existence.

Possession helps the creature in us feel secure. Some people like to possess things; some like to possess people, while others cling to images or ideas.

But we best forsake these things for the perfection and freedom of nothingness. As Jesus said, 'Whoever would save their soul must lose it.'

We must even forsake 'God', as only thoughts and images can gather round labels. God is happy that we should leave in this way; for direct experience sees without labels

So, today notice the creature in yourself, with its desire to possess things, people, images or ideas. And take leave of your desires, for all are diminished and entrapped by them, both desirer and desired.

Such abandonment is the highest death;
and it leaves us with nothing to present
to others except our freedom.

How Will We Know?

How will I know when dawn breaks?
You will see through to the innocence of others.

How will I know when dawn breaks?
You will move in the world more freely.

How will I know when dawn breaks?
You will notice yourself more clearly.

How will I know when dawn breaks?
You will exist in the world more generously.

How will I know when dawn breaks?
You will suffer in the world more lightly.

How will I know when dawn breaks?

*When you accept the night as a
friend, dawn has already broken.*

Mapu and the Angel

This story is told of Mapu and the angel.

Mapu lived happily in a village selling fruit in the market. One day, the angel Khabir appeared to him and told him to jump in the fast-flowing river.

Mapu did this immediately and was carried downstream until someone threw him a rope and pulled him out. This same man offered him a job in his fishing business. Mapu was grateful to accept and worked for the man for a few happy years until the angel told him to move on again.

After passing through a few villages, Mapu got work in a fabric shop, learning this new craft relatively happily until the angel appeared again and sent him on his way. Down the years, Mapu worked in various jobs in this manner, always moving on when instructed by the angel.

By the time Mapu was an old man, he'd gained a reputation for being compassionate and wise and people came to him with their problems. One day, a visitor said, 'Mapu, how did you get to where you are now?' Mapu thought for a moment and replied: 'It's difficult to say, really.'

It was difficult to say because Mapu's only skill was to listen to the angel Khabir, whose name means 'The All Aware'; his only skill was openness to the instruction of awareness and the courage to act on what he heard.

May such openness and courage be yours.

ABOUT THE AUTHOR

 **Simon Parke** has worked with the NHS, social services and European banks in staff support and personal development. He is CEO of The Mind Clinic, which takes mindful listening into the work place.

Simon has written extensively, with award-winning scripts for TV and radio and a trilogy of murder mysteries. He runs, leads retreats, has recently moved to the south coast – and follows the beautiful game too closely.

www.simonparke.com

CPSIA information can be obtained
at www.ICGtesting.com
Printed in the USA
FSOW01n0542070515
6950FS